ONE PERSON
ACTED
and *Everything* CHANGED

ONE PERSON
ACTED
and *Everything* CHANGED

10 Inspiring Accounts of World Changers

DEBORAH ROHAN
with Ricky Schlueter

ROHAN
BOOKS

ONE PERSON ACTED AND EVERYTHING CHANGED

Library of Congress Control Number: 2016943951

ISBN (Print) 978-0-692-60238-6

This book is dedicated to my daughter,

Jessica.

Your lifelong dedication to protecting the voiceless has influenced me in more ways than I could tally or express. You, too, are a world changer extraordinaire, and I would not have experienced the world with as broad a lens or depth of meaning without your graceful leadership, gentle nudges, and unconditional love. For that I am eternally grateful.

"The opposite of hope is action."

Joanna Macy

CONTENTS

Foreword

By Jack Canfield

If you have ever wondered whether you are one of those chosen few able to truly engender change and make the world better, this book will answer your question. Be ready to act, however, because I can tell you already the answer is a strong and unquestionable, YES!

How do I know this without knowing you? My life's work of over forty years has revealed this lesson thousands of times over. As a world leader in teaching transformation and peak performance strategies, and as the author of more than 66 best selling books including *The Success Principles*™ and the *Chicken Soup for the Soul*® Series, I have been teaching individuals they can accomplish anything if they are clear about their purpose, if they know exactly what they want to accomplish, if they take action, and if they persist in the face of great and multiple challenges. That's exactly what the ten world changers in this book have done against formidable odds, and the results are at once extraordinary and inspiring, even to me!

The back stories and inspiration that author Deborah Rohan details in these deeply personal stories will challenge your perception of what one motivated person can accomplish. Regardless of background, gender, color, religion, country of origin, or level of education, the individuals in this riveting book demonstrate with their lives how deep passion, clarity of purpose, and hard work trump everything else, whether your dreams are modest or seemingly impossible. Whether one is lifting millions of individuals out of poverty worldwide, changing the future for girls in Liberia from prostitution to getting world-class educations, ending egregious abuse of farmed animals, saving our oceans from ultimate collapse, and so much more, when one person acts, indeed, everything can and does change.

What the ten individuals in this book have accomplished is more than many governments have been able to do. Without waiting for permission or expecting 'someone else' to fix things, they decided if change was going to happen, it would be up to them to make it so.

Their results are quite literally life-changing and often life-saving; they are indeed world-changing, and they provide us solid and irrefutable evidence that each of us is powerful beyond our wildest dreams.

When I first met Deborah, she had been devoting her own life to changing the world by bringing diverse and sometimes warring people together in dialogue and shared experiences. She attended one of my weeklong trainings on success, later became a *Canfield Success Principles Trainer*, and has since built a company that provides inspiration and training to individuals and organizations eager to bring about meaningful change of their own. With this moving and sometimes shocking book, she honors those who gain courage and self-belief as they act in service to the world, and inspires those who wonder if they still can.

As the personal stories of each person in this book so beautifully illustrate, the journey truly is the destination. No one can act so boldly and remain the same. It is now impossible for each of them to ungrow, unlearn, or turn back, and it will be the same for you. Should you take on your own endeavor, you will, in time, arrive in an entirely new place, one of deep satisfaction and enhanced connection with the rest of the world. It is a privilege reserved for those of vision, courage, and action.

I applaud you for taking the first step and gaining inspiration and knowledge from this book. I join Deborah in encouraging you to continue on and take that leap of faith, believe in yourself enough to join these ten world changers, and make this world better in whatever small or grand way makes you come alive.

To your success in making a better world for all of us,

Jack Canfield.

Internationally recognized leader in personal development, and author or co-author of more than 150 books, including The Success Principles™ and the Chicken Soup for the Soul®Series.

Santa Barbara, California.

Introduction

For the average reader, this sentence will take about four seconds to read. During those four seconds, we lost a lot of our world's rainforest—roughly 8 football stadiums worth. Experts tell us that this assault on our rainforests has a sobering consequence: we're losing nearly 140 plant and animal species every single day.

In this age of information, we are constantly made aware of tragic situations the world over. We read about them in newspapers and online, we hear about them from friends and co-workers, we watch them unfold on television. We know that something has to change—we may even feel compelled to help change it ourselves—but when the complexity and enormity of the situation sinks in, it can be paralyzing. Without even taking our first step, we start accepting defeat. "I'm just one person. I cannot possibly change this." These self-imposed limits seem rational. It isn't reasonable to expect one person to be able to affect, let alone dramatically change, these lopsided situations. After all, a pebble can't stop a wave.

Except that it can, and in fact, it is the only thing that can and the only thing that ever will. The second stone can only come after the first. This book is about the first pebble—the puissant pioneer —who ignored the odds and broke the wave.

It was a young woman named Katie Meyler who first jolted me awake and convinced me that the only thing holding us back from creating a world that works for all of us is our individual and collective mindset. Following her journey over the past several years has entirely reshaped my concept of how each of us can change the world.

In this book you will read about Katie's evolution from a 22-year old New Jersey girl with a community college education, piles of student loans, shaky self confidence and a burdened childhood whose raw passion for helping people vaulted her far beyond the limitations that could easily have defined her life. Because she resolutely refused to accept that little girls in a Liberian slum should be forced to sell their bodies to survive, in just seven years Katie morphed from a fast food worker into a leader who is changing the future of Liberia's youth. Today she meets with Liberian President Ellen Sirleaf Johnson, first lady Michelle Obama, billionaire businessman Warren Buffet and many others in her work to change the options for destitute girls in Liberia from prostitution to education.

While following Katie and the stunning accomplishments she was achieving in Liberia, I began to notice others refusing to accept a status quo they found untenable. Like Nathan Runkle, who, as an eleven-year old boy growing up in rural Ohio, believed the way animals were being treated on factory farms was an anathema. He was an island of dissent within a sea of ranchers, yet he listened only to the calling of his own soul and by the age of fifteen founded a non-profit to change the way farmed animals are raised. Sixteen years later, Mercy for Animals is a worldwide force for compassion that has transformed the treatment of millions of farmed animals in 90 countries by exposing cruelty, forcing changes in corporate policy, proposing protective legislation, and educating the public about the many reasons to choose a plant-based diet.

The *awakening* that tells us we each hold a power inside us that is far beyond what we know or imagine is not limited to the naiveté of youth— those who don't yet know what they don't know. There are visionaries who discovered their passion to create change in the course of carrying out their chosen profession, then made something akin to a U-turn in their life's work. Like Paul Polak, who in his work as a psychiatrist for more than twenty-three years noticed a strong correlation between psychiatric trauma and poverty, and for the next thirty-plus years worked to extinguish global poverty. He has since helped millions of people move themselves out of poverty in fourteen developing nations and is the driving force behind a movement encouraging big business to help finish the job.

Louie Psihoyos had an enviable 17-year career as a staff photographer for National Geographic. Traveling to exotic locations worldwide, thrilling readers with exquisite photographs, and impacting change by highlighting social problems, he surrendered that life when he could no longer ignore the degradation of coral reefs in his favorite scuba diving spots. Having witnessed firsthand the toll fossil fuels unleash on the environment from stories he'd covered, he gave up his coveted position at National Geographic to make films and dramatic visual productions that educate the world on the urgency of saving our dying oceans and disappearing species.

One million times a month, people around the world ask Google how to change the world. I find solace in that because more than any time in our history, the world needs changing. Katie Meyler may have been the first pebble for me, but the real impetus for this book comes from my fundamental belief that those million people a month can save the world if only they believed in their ability to do so. I want to show people that no matter their circumstances, their education, their economic status, or their location, if they want to change the world, they can. My hope is that they do. My hope is that we all do.

Deborah Rohan

KATIE MEYLER
Founder, More than Me Foundation

GETTING GIRLS OFF THE STREETS & INTO THE CLASSROOM IN LIBERIA, WEST AFRICA

"I want to shake the earth in a way that says, 'What are we living for?
Are we living for something bigger than ourselves?'
Normal people can do really, really big things."

Young, uneducated girls in Liberia, West Africa, suffer from extreme poverty, sexual exploitation, and chronic hunger, but they do have something to be grateful for: a rambunctious, endlessly passionate young American wonder woman named Katie Meyler who is restoring their hope and changing their future.

Katie grew up in a desperately poor home smack in the middle of a drug-infested, New Jersey neighborhood. She thought of herself as "not smart," inadequately educated, and unlikely to go far in life. Instead, she found a way to break all societal inequities and self-imposed limits. Summoning the courage to travel to Liberia in her early twenties, she discovered an entire generation of youth whose desperation eclipsed her own complaints, giving her the courage to fight for their future. By the age of 30, she would open a school to educate young girls otherwise destined to survive by prostitution, if they survived at all. In the process, she would fight the scourge of Ebola, later to be recognized for her efforts as one of *Time Magazine*'s Persons of the Year, return hope to people living in one of the world's most notorious slums, and quite literally change the future of education and health for the entire country of Liberia.

In so doing, Katie found her passion and her voice; and in Katie's case, both are as raw and real as it gets. The best way to understand her authenticity is to listen to the spoken-word poetry she fervently delivers whenever she gets the opportunity. Her audiences range from a small group of desperate onlookers standing on the garbage-strewn streets of West Point (the giant slum on the outskirts of Monrovia), to the Women of the United Nations, from leaders of the Fortune 400, to—most recently—First Lady, Michelle Obama. No matter the audience, Katie is pure Katie.

She Is My Promise is a powerful example of Katie's spoken word poetry. Recorded early on in her efforts to "do something" to save the young, at-risk girls in the Liberian slum, it reveals her anguish when she cannot find Abigail, an eleven-year old girl Katie had been trying to get off the streets and into school.

She is My Promise

So I'm back on this bathroom floor again
And it's the middle of the night again,
and flashes of your face keep me up again.
It's you Abigail
You have stained my soul.
Is it a street worker?
Is it a sex worker?
You tell me,
What is the politically correct way to say that
My eleven-year old friend, Abigail
Is a war-orphaned prostitute?
Yes, this two-dollar hooker,
This child,
She opens her legs to men
So that she can stay alive
And right now,
I'm not sure if she is alive.
And when I think about her
I don't have the words to describe.
My friend, Abigail, is missing.
She is gone.
She is nowhere to be found.
And when I call her name
Nobody knows her.
Her community tells me matter of factly, "she's vanished."
Her country shushes me. It's not good for their reputation.
My country tells me it's not polite to talk about her.
Here, she is the blame of a corrupt government in a country
That people know nothing about.
Here, she is just another abstract thought that would never

cross someone's mind
On a line to purchase a cup of coffee
That costs more than she would make
Selling her body for one day.
Here she is just another Facebook cause
That people check they like, because it's trendy
Or because they are too lazy to do anything else about it.
She is the bottom of the earth
To a world that has been brutal to her
That has beat her up and raped her in ways that
People who could read would never be able to pronounce.
Now this small child is gone,
And I promised her I would come and find her
And I can't.
So I'm up again
On this bathroom floor again
And it's the middle of the night again
And I need to scream her name.
Abigail! Where are you?
I'm trying to find you.
I haven't forgotten you!
I am struggling to find words
To talk about you
People here are offended by you
Disturbed by you.
I am too.
You keep me up at night
And I hope that you always do.
You are my vow
My promise.
I'm coming to get you.

If Katie Meyler was ever an average person, she left any evidence of that in the rear view mirror a long time ago. She moves through the day with a life force that mesmerizes. If you can imagine an open, playful, gigantic heart stuffed into a person seemingly too small to contain it all, so that pieces of her spirit are zapping out from all parts of her in a way she cannot control, you have an idea of her essence. Her eyes are brilliantly lit and dancing; her voice full of emotion and range, and when she releases a torrent of spoken word poetry so haunting in truth and power it is as if she is channeling Rumi and Maya Angelou combined. Her body moves in a rhythm so uninhibited that she frequently bounces about and occasionally breaks into dance.

A recent Facebook post catches this fervor perfectly, and it's one reason she has become a masterful fundraiser: "Totally just walked up to a table from *Coca-Cola Liberia* & performed a poem. The marketing manager and the CSR woman were there and they say they'll help us!"

A natural and savvy marketer, Katie seizes every opportunity. The next post she placed on her Facebook page was a photo of six girls enrolled in her newly-opened school, *More than Me Academy*, dancing beneath a huge Coca-Cola sign. She was preparing to send the photo off to her new friends at *Coca Cola Liberia* to bolster her plea for funds.

In a powerful one two punch, the next post on Katie's Facebook page included a link to a BBC article titled, "Liberian Students **ALL** Fail University Admission Exam."

While one might assume this was a typo or written in a misleading manner, the linked BBC article clearly stated: "Nearly 25,000 school-leavers failed the test for admission to the University of Liberia, one of two state-run universities. It means that the overcrowded university will not have any new first-year students when it reopens next month for the academic year." Clearly, Katie picked a challenge as large and improbable in scope as her bold enthusiasm.

AN UNLIKELY BEGINNING

"You cannot kill these boys! I am going to call the United Nations."

Katie Meyler started life with a myriad of crushing disadvantages. In addition to living in an impoverished home in a rough neighborhood, she was regularly beaten by her abusive, alcoholic father, and repeatedly watched her drug-addicted sister be rushed to the emergency room for crack overdoses. Her mother, a fervently religious, Pentecostal Christian, worked the graveyard shift at a local factory earning minimum wage, leaving Katie with a television set as her babysitter. Life was a brutal, daily struggle, but a deep-seated resilience allowed her to claw her way through school and eventually earn a degree at a community college.

So how did a gangly, 23-year-old Jersey girl with a bushel of student loans and a rough upbringing find her way to Liberia, lift children out of prostitution, open a school, fill it with computers and other necessities, help lead the community through the Ebola crisis, and be asked by the president of the country to help guide and design the educational future of Liberia?

"I just feel there were all these miracles along the way. And I hate to say that because people who are just starting projects will ask, 'How do I know miracles will happen?' But I think part of the miracle is that you just work your ass off and you start attracting people. When you work that hard it eventually pays off." Whether by example or coaching, her mother's religious beliefs resulted in Katie volunteering to help with a church-sponsored adult literacy program in Liberia in 2006, just three years after the second of two brutal civil wars ended. Liberia's infrastructure was decimated, and poverty levels were (and remain) deep and intractable, with the country routinely ranked among the top five poorest countries in the world. Amidst the ongoing wars, an estimated 340,000 children were orphaned, leaving them prey to every possible negative outcome including forced military recruitment by the armies of neighboring countries, and for utter survival, prostitution. Prostitution is very common in Liberia; even married women use it to sustain their lives, often with their husband's blessing.

During her time tutoring adults in Monrovia, Katie briefly helped a crew filming a documentary in neighboring West Point, one of the most dangerous and tuberculosis-afflicted slums in the world.

"It's a very rough area. The photographers were even afraid to take out their cameras because they thought they would be stolen."

The level of poverty struck her profoundly. "You can't go to West Point and not be changed for life."

West Point is home to more than 80,000 people with no electricity, no running water, and only four public toilets for the entire population. Residents live as close to one another as humanly possible. Their homes are made from corrugated metal, built inches apart from each other, each housing an average of six people.

As the film crew began their work, Katie noticed a young girl following her. She was darting between rows of tin shacks, peeking out to watch Katie's every move. At the end of the day the girl ran up and tugged on Katie's shirt.

"Can you come and see my mom?"

The 8-year old girl led Katie to her makeshift home, a warehouse used to store charcoal. She and her mother slept on the cement floor of the warehouse, living as squatters with no blankets and no clothes beyond those they wore. The little girl told Katie she and her mother survived by begging for food. Katie saw immediately that the girl's mother was behaving in a psychotic manner, seemingly out of touch with reality.

They were the first people Katie met and among those she will never forget.

When Katie's volunteer church mission ended, she didn't feel ready to leave Liberia. She had come to consider the children she had met in the slums as friends and felt desperate to help them improve their lives.

Katie convinced the church to let her remain in Liberia alone. She promised she would work to raise money through the church organization and to find some way to help the Liberian people.

She found affordable housing in a local residence where visiting missionaries paid $200 per month for rent. It provided a safe harbor and bought her time. She knew no one in the country but anyone who has met Katie knows she cannot remain friendless for long. When passing through the lobby of the Liberia Royal Hotel one afternoon, she spotted a preppy-looking American looking decidedly out of place. She approached him, learned his name was Josh, and discovered he was a recent graduate of Cornell University volunteering in Liberia for the summer. Not only would he become her best friend and mentor, his advice would eventually change her future forever.

Each night during his stay in Liberia Josh set up a free, mini-library for the community outside his temporary home in the West Point slum. It was a beautiful act that touched Katie deeply. She was taken with his compassion for these people who had endured unimaginable atrocities, and they bonded over their love for the Liberian people.

One evening, a large and angry crowd gathered near Josh's home where Katie was having dinner. The sounds from the mob were deafening, growing so loud and violent that Katie hid in the closet, fearing for her life. She desperately grabbed at clothes to hide herself. Josh took a candle and went outside to investigate.

When Josh hadn't returned after ten minutes, Katie could no longer stay put and emerged from her hiding spot to look for him. There is no public lighting in the West Point slums, and thus the streets were dark, save a few hand-held candles and flashlights. The deafening noise led her toward a very large group of people gathered in a circle, all yelling and swinging machetes, occasionally pausing to sharpen them on the gravel. This massive group of adult men and women were hailing stones onto two teenage boys huddled in the center of the circle, intent on stoning the terrified boys to death.

Katy snuck up behind the violent masses just as they began to beat the boys with sticks and cut them with machetes. The security guards stationed nearby were watching and laughing, doing nothing to stop the mob attack. Mortified, Katie forgot her fear and jumped into the middle of the circle and began screaming, "You cannot kill these boys! I am going to call the United Nations!" At once the crowd stopped, and started laughing at her.

"But truly, because I am American, they listened to me. And they stopped. It was amazing."

Katie and Josh were able to retrieve a few soldiers from a UN peacekeeping force stationed nearby. As they held the boys and waited for the UN soldiers, a man in the crowd told her, "If you lived here, and you were Liberian, you would also want these boys killed."

It was a night Katie learned about the local culture in a way she would never forget. The man explained that the boys had been sneaking into houses and stealing things. The West Point slum was a place where people use sheets for front doors. No one uses banks and their meager possessions were available for the taking. The boys had been stealing from their own community. Katie learned that mob violence was the only means to justice and to stopping thieves that the community had available to them. Not only did these and other boys steal, they often killed people, sometimes only to take an article of clothing a person was wearing. If these boys were set free, the man explained, they would be back and may even kill children if they get in their way. There was no other form of justice, no police force. When summer ended and it came time for Josh to return to the United States to attend law school, Katie continued on alone. She wasn't sure what she could do to alter the deplorable situation but she deeply believed she could help in some way, even if the exact path remained unclear.

Josh told her, "You are doing amazing work here, playing with the kids, helping out families. But when you leave, they will still be poor. They will still be hungry. What can you do to change that?"

"I don't know yet," she told him.He left her what cash he had—a few hundred dollars—to help with her efforts. She used the money to pay school fees for seven of the children as there was no free public education available.

HELP ALONG THE WAY

"One day, after placing my pee in the refrigerator, I posted on the local Couch Surfing site, 'Peeing in the Fridge to Save the World – Help!'"

After Josh left, Katie met a Jamaican-born corporate tax attorney named Erica who lived in New York City. Once a year she spent one month volunteering for *Lawyers without Borders* in Liberia. One afternoon she spotted Katie on the beach in West Point playing with a group of kids. She approached Katie to learn what she was doing in Liberia and the chance meeting quickly developed into a friendship.

Katie was building her network one person at a time, yet had no idea she was doing so. From the Liberian man who first introduced her to the West Point slum, to Josh, and now Erica, Katie was gathering support for her efforts to help the children of Liberia move from prostitution to education.

Before long, Katie ran out of money and knew she had to come up with a serious plan. Somewhat disheartened, she returned home to New Jersey hoping she might be able to start some kind of an organization to help these kids in Liberia find a better future.

Back in New York, she reconnected with Erica who told her, "Katie, you are full of passion, full of ideas, great with these kids. Why don't you start your own non-profit foundation, and I'll help do the paperwork?" Katie said she was in, but for what, she had literally no idea.

Katie and Erica came up with a working mission: "Something to give opportunities, give dreams to the most desperate kids in developing countries." Katie laughs about the absolute vagueness of her original mission now.

"It was very, very broad. I was only 23 and I didn't know anything!"

That initial discussion with Erica started to fade as Katie had no idea where to start on such a project. Meanwhile she found a job working at Times Square Red Lobster selling frozen biscuits and seafood to tourists.

"I had no idea what to do with my life. I was applying to development agencies, just hoping to find a job helping people. I just wanted to help people!" With barely an acorn of an idea, Katie decided to take a drive to the University of Michigan where Josh was attending law school. He understood her passion for the children of Liberia as no one else could and she thought he might have some advice.

She told him, "I want to start a non-profit organization, but I just don't think I have what it takes to run a foundation. I didn't go to an Ivy League college like you did. I barely know how to use a comma. There are mounds and mounds of paperwork to apply for a non-profit status and it's a year-long process to even launch the thing. I don't even know how or where to begin. I don't even know what a board of directors is."

Josh leaned forward and looked directly at Katie. He didn't mince words. "Katie, get the f… over yourself. It's not about you."

Her eyes flew open. She was stunned at his directness but it was exactly what she needed to hear. "He was right. It was hard to think of myself as being capable of pulling it off. Although I believed I was a leader, I didn't think I was smart, and that was a huge insecurity for me. The truth is that I am smart; I just didn't read much then. When you start reading, you realize that's the way you learn things in the world. And when you are curious, and find something you love, that's an incentive to investigate the world.

"I had a nine-hour drive back to New York, and in my head the whole time I kept hearing Josh's words, 'It's not about you… it's not about you.' Again and again. And that's when I got the name for the organization: More than Me."

After that revelation struck, Katie's passion found some focus. She knew she wanted to start living for something bigger than herself. And one by one, people appeared in her life, willing to help.

She met a web designer named Francesco from Italy, who helped her put together a business plan for More than Me. He designed the web site and paid for many of the initial expenses.

She met again with Erica, the lawyer she met in Liberia, who wrote and filed the application for the 501c3 non-profit status with the IRS.

"It's not only Katie Meyler who did this!" she insists. "There were so many people that, if they hadn't come along, More than Me wouldn't be here."

Back at her job at Red Lobster, Katie's enthusiasm for her fledgling organization was contagious. "I was so excited about it I was telling customers, and they became so excited they wanted to donate even before we got the charity going. They would buy books for me and bring them to me to help me along. One of the books was *Blue like Jazz*. It's about a man who truly cares about the world. One of the opening sentences says, 'I never really liked jazz music before. But this one time I was standing on a bridge, and I saw this man playing the saxophone. And his eyes were closed for thirty minutes as he played. After that, I loved jazz music.'

"Sometimes, you have to see someone else loving something before you can love it. You love it through them. I think that's the case with More than Me. People might really be able to relate to these girls in Liberia because they see and feel *my* passion and love for them."

Katie didn't think she could raise much money until she received the IRS non-profit status. Though she was working at Red Lobster to pay her bills, she was restless waiting. One night she was lying in bed watching an Oprah rerun at 2 a.m. and saw a young man named Craig Kielburger who had started an organization called *Free the Children*. She was immediately drawn in by his passion to help children around the world who were being forced into hard labor at young ages. The next day she sent in an application to *Free the Children*, offering to do anything... filing... mailroom... clean up ... she didn't care. She told them she simply needed to be around the work they were doing.

Apparently Katie's passion shows through on paper, too, because she was offered an incredible opportunity. "Would you be interested in being an 'Oprah Ambassador?'" they asked. Oprah's Angel Network and Free the Children had teamed up, and they needed motivational speakers to talk to children around the country. As a person who jumps—not merely responds—but *jumps* on an opportunity, Katie began training to become a professional speaker. Over the next eight months, as she awaited an answer about her non-profit status, she traveled across the U.S. and shared her story of growing up among drugs and poverty in New Jersey.

On August 14, 2009, just two months after her speaking tour ended, the letter arrived. More than Me was officially recognized by the U. S. government as a non-profit organization.

"I was screaming with joy! The entire neighborhood heard me!

"So there I was. I had the 501c3 non-profit status, but I still had no money. No salary. I knew I could raise money, but I had no track record to speak of. And I knew absolutely nothing about fundraising. I worked my ass off to raise $2,000. Now I laugh at that, but then people would ask me, 'How old are you? 26? How many kids are you helping put in school? Only seven?' Yeah, they really didn't want to get behind me on that one."

The following two years reveal much about Katie's personality, zeal, courage, and absolute dedication to her mission. Eager to start raising money and launching More than Me, and wanting to do so far from the oppressive neighborhood where she grew up, Katie turned to Couch Surfing, a program that connects travelers across the world and provides a free place to stay in strangers' homes. More than that, Couch Surfing is a community in itself, and Katie credits that community with helping her launch More than Me.

To pay her bills, which consisted of student loans, phone bills, food and travel for fundraising, she performed a series of jobs, many of which clearly fall under the "odd" category. In addition to substitute teaching and cleaning roof gutters, she began renting her body out to pharmaceutical companies for experiments. She later upgraded to the National Institute for Health in Washington, D.C., who offered a free place to live and a $1,500 a month stipend so they could test how air affects metabolism. Placed inside a room resembling a space ship, she was handed drinks through a small door.

"I had to collect my pee and put it in the refrigerator—and you know they can see you doing it. They also took blood through these holes in the room. And they kept taking blood, and taking more blood."One day, after placing my pee in the refrigerator, I posted on the local Couch Surfing site, 'Peeing in the Fridge to Save the World—Help!'" She wrote that she had just started a non-profit organization to help kids go to school in Africa, and if anyone was interested they should meet her for coffee.

"So many people showed up to help! On that one day alone, a woman with a master's degree in Non-Profit Management and a man who worked at a corporate non-profit showed up to meet and talk."

The woman, Stephanie Hood, jumped in with both feet. "Stephanie started helping me with a plan and introduced me to others in Washington, D.C., and they started helping me. Stephanie was one of the hardest working people I ever met. She worked full time and donated all her spare time to More than Me. She had been a community organizer for Obama and really knew her stuff. I also met a guy at a coffee shop who ended up being a web designer. He introduced me to some funders, and then we just put together a group in D.C. to put the thing together. People just always materialized to help the process go forward."

Eventually Katie raised enough money to travel back to Liberia to reconnect with the young girls she had been helping financially, as well as to plot a new course. While the travel funds solved one financial piece she had no money to live on.

Desperate for an answer, she made a tough decision. She would sell her ovarian eggs. Not once, but twice.

"It's not an easy process," she stresses. "Not at all. It involves blood tests, and giving yourself shots every day for weeks, and then a surgical procedure to remove the eggs. That's just part of it."

It was a big decision, and yet she had to live, had to pay her bills, and had to pay to stay in Liberia. Eventually, she would need to move there to develop More than Me. It all cost money.

Once back in Liberia, she met up with the man who had first shown her around the ghetto of West Point. Together they studied the situation and discovered that almost three-quarters of youth in the entire country of Liberia were not attending school at all. Out of that disturbing figure, 80% were girls. So together they made a decision to focus their energy on educating girls because they were the ones most at risk for sexual exploitation. They also knew that when an investment is made in a girl's education, everyone in the community is likely to benefit.

AN INCREDIBLE JOURNEY

"Would you give a dollar to get your neighbor off the street? Would you give four quarters for your friend, for your sister, for your daughter, so that she could stay off the street for that day?"

With a small scholarship program developed, Katie's next step was opening a tuition-free school for girls, as much to get them off the streets as to educate them. Her chance came in 2012 when she used her natural instincts and social media prowess to bring More than Me before American eyes and hearts. By creating a powerful, tear-inducing, video titled *I am Abigail*, she drove home the fact that the girls who become prostitutes, like her young friend Abigail who earned $1 a day, could be any of us.

"Think about that," Katie commands on the video filled with the flashing faces of ten-year old girls. "Would you give a dollar to get your neighbor off the street? Would you give four quarters for your friend, for your sister, for your daughter, so that she could stay off the street for that day? This is a poverty issue, this is a women's and girl's issue, it's an injustice issue, this is a health issue, but more than anything, this is a people issue. Abigail is a person. And she could be you. She could be me. I'm not even asking you for money. I'm just asking for your vote."

With that powerful video Katie and her volunteer staff launched a massive Facebook campaign, asking people to send in photos of themselves with the words "I am Abigail" written across their foreheads. She then posted hundreds of photos from around the world, showing global concern for the cause. She also asked people to vote for More than Me in NBC's *American Giving Awards* sponsored by the JP Morgan Chase Foundation.

When the night came for the winners to be announced on a televised special, and Katie heard the words "More than Me" announced as the first place winner of one million dollars, she very nearly fainted. With "I Am Abigail" scrawled across her forehead in black marker, she gave a tearful yet powerful, off-the-cuff thank you speech that brought even greater attention to her fledgling non-profit organization.

Though the money wouldn't arrive in a lump sum, the annual amount provided More than Me the opportunity to move from a scholarship program to opening a school. The President of Liberia, Ellen Sirleaf Johnson, told Katie, "We have plenty of empty government buildings you can choose from. They are all bombed and looted, but you can have one." With the help of a local business, the chosen building was restored, and made suitable for a school.

In August of 2013, Liberia's only tuition-free, all-girls school opened its doors for the first time with 124 girls in grades K-4. The students received two nutritious meals a day, and stayed engaged and off the streets from 7 am to 5 pm. To Katie, it felt like an absolute miracle.

Girls are greeted by their new teacher on their first day of school—ever.

All was right with the world. Abigail, the missing girl in Katie's spoken poetry, and focus of the fundraising campaign, was indeed found, and was among those lucky girls who started school that first day More than Me Academy opened. The future looked bright for the girls of Liberia. The girls were emerging from their shyness and apprehension, and were beginning to understand that their lives were about to change in a very good way.

CATASTROPHE STRIKES

"Children were lying all alone next to dead bodies. Literally, dead people outside the hospital, dead people inside the hospital, mixed with people who were alive. It was chaos."

Sometimes being a leader means switching gears, handling emergencies, and finding order out of chaos. Sometimes it gets a lot worse than that.

With the school humming along, Katie returned to the United States to engage in public relations and fund raising. With a powerful story to tell, Katie, who had become a passionate and skilled speaker, began spreading the message of the importance of educating girls. She told the story of her journey, of the girls' ongoing development from hopeless lives to bright futures, and of the massive need for more schools across Liberia. She spoke to corporations, schools, businesses, and to the Fortune 400, where she met and mesmerized one the world's richest men, Warren Buffet.

So taken with Katie's work in Liberia, Warren Buffet kneels and offers a mock proposal.

It was sometime in August, 2014, less than a year after More than Me Academy opened, when Katie got the news. The deadly Ebola virus was moving into Liberia. Continuing her fundraising efforts in the United States, Katie followed the news and spoke to the staff daily. The epidemic spiked quickly, and when she saw a news story about panic and rioting breaking out in West Point, where most of their students lived, she knew she needed to return. Though nearly all other foreigners, journalists, aid workers, diplomats, and even native Liberians were fleeing Liberia as fast as they could, Katie knew her girls and her staff needed her. Despite desperate pleas from her mother, family, friends, and others to not go into harm's way, she hopped on a plane, flew to Monrovia, and walked directly into the Ebola storm.

The Ebola outbreak was so widespread and deadly that it would completely redefine the West Point slums, Liberia as a whole, as well as much of North and Western Africa. It would change Katie forever. When the highly contagious nature of the virus became apparent, schools across the entire nation were closed. Indefinitely.

Ignoring a strict quarantine, Katie marched directly into the West Point slum to meet with the leaders she had come to know well over the years. She wanted to learn what was happening and what gaps in response and health care needed filling. The school was closed, but she knew More than Me could do something to help.

"We met with all the people who worked in West Point. The Ministry of Health hadn't paid many of the workers yet. So we paid them. The people who were going door to door looking for Ebola patients didn't have boots. So we bought 300 pairs of boots. We discovered it was taking up to five days for ambulances to arrive to transport the sick and dying to the hospitals and treatment centers. So one of my donors sent me money and we bought an ambulance."

With the hospital filled beyond capacity, there was nowhere to put those who were infected as they awaited treatment. Katie walked through a holding center that was set up to accommodate those waiting for admission. She was mortified by what she saw. Patients were lying alone, scared and suffering, with no contact allowed between them and their loved ones.

"Children were lying all alone next to dead bodies. Literally, dead people outside the hospital, dead people inside the hospital, mixed with people who were alive. It was chaos."

Ambulances arrived steadily, often with corpses who had been alive when they were picked up. As she would later report to a *Time Magazine* correspondent, "It was horror. It was hell on earth.""I watched a woman die in front of me in a taxi waiting to go into the hospital. In the meantime, a truck pulls up. The truck is Red Cross, and they're coming to collect dead bodies. They opened up the gates in the hospital, and they're taking one dead body after the next dead body and putting them in the truck. Everyone was screaming and crying. I was crying, and then I started laughing, just because it was, like, so overwhelming. I was, like, breaking, in a way."

The carnage would continue unabated for seven months before the number of deaths began to stabilize and slowly decline. During those months, More than Me transported 262 people suspected of having Ebola; their nursing team visited nearly 3,000 homes and donated food and other items to over 100 of them. They educated over 14,000 residents on how to protect themselves from the fast moving disease. Their social workers counseled survivors and provided them with financial, psychological, and emotional help to reintegrate them back into society, as many were being shunned by friends and even family members who feared they might still be contagious. Regardless of the brave face Katie wore, it was a horrendous experience. From the time she became ill and had to be tested for Ebola, (it was negative), to the death of so many good friends, to the absolute anguish of watching a young girl named Sarah, who she knew well and dearly loved, walk alone into the clinic and never return, to dealing with scores of broken families and more orphans than she could bear, Katie continued on, and so did her staff.

Katie is the first to share credit and says she didn't do it alone. The More than Me staff, including their nurse, local community volunteers, those who sent large and small donations from across the world, her board of directors, and so many others took extensive and even drastic measures to help the decimated community.

Finally, on March 2, 2015, More than Me Academy officially reopened, and two months later the World Health Organization declared Liberia free of Ebola transmission.

A SHINING BEACON OF HOPE

Educationally, they are thriving. In July of 2015, More than Me students won first place in the citywide spelling bee in the capital city of Monrovia, beating out 24 other schools.

Today More than Me Academy is a shining beacon of hope in Liberia. Students are receiving stellar educations, learning about life, building self-esteem, and setting challenging life goals for themselves. They love school so much they attend before and after school programs and often stay well into the evening. Students receive psychological support, health care and nutritional guidance, engage in an extensive art program, take computer classes, receive vocational training, and simply relax in an atmosphere of support and love.

Katie and her colleagues wanted to accomplish many things with More than Me. The most critically important was getting and keeping girls off the streets and away from sexual exploitation. Providing them with a basic education and helping them become literate was next. Helping them realize they have choices in life by raising their belief in themselves, and by harnessing their inner power, both individually and collectively, was of paramount importance and has been enormously life changing already.

When More than Me Academy first opened its doors not one of the girls had set foot inside a school before. Now, just three years later, having survived the worst of the Ebola crisis, and with thirty students who lost some or all of their family members, the More than Me community continues to thrive with incredible momentum.

Radiant smiles adorn More than Me students celebrating their spelling bee victory.

Academically, the students are thriving. In July of 2015, More than Me students won first place in the citywide spelling bee in the capital city of Monrovia, beating out 24 other schools.

As President Sirleaf Johnson, the first female leader of an African country, said: "Give them an education. That's what this program [More than Me] is all about. To expand Katie Meyler's initiative to as many communities across the country as possible, and get all those young girls in school learning to become professionals."

To that end, work is currently underway to expand the More than Me model nation-wide across Liberia, and Katie Meyler is front and center, leading the charge.

LOOKING FORWARD AND REFLECTING BACK

"But a leader isn't someone who isn't afraid. A leader is someone who is afraid and acts anyway."

It is likely that the rapid pace at which More than Me developed could only have happened with someone as dynamic and uninhibited as Katie Meyler. While she felt she didn't know what she was doing or how to do it, the speed with which progress unfolded has been nothing short of extraordinary. She didn't know she would move hearts, succeed in her mission, or change the face of a community, and eventually, the future of an entire country.

"The beginning is the hard part. Now we are about to explode—in a *good* way. At first no one believes in you, so you have to believe in yourself. You have to prove yourself. Once you've done that, it gets easier."

Recently she joined others from Liberia's Ministry of Education and Shelter for Life, an NGO also working in the country, to travel across Liberia to study how they might fix the education system nationwide. Visiting two government schools in every county in Liberia, they found impassable roads, schools with no books, desks, or chairs, and many without roofs. They skipped one county all together because the roads were flat out unusable.

Almost immediately upon their return to the capital, Katie and the others each gave a presentation of their findings to an assembled group of luminaries. Among the audience eager to hear their thoughts on Liberia's educational needs were the President of Liberia, the country's ministers, the head of the World Bank, the head of the Monetary Fund, a host of ambassadors to and from Liberia, and several other dignitaries all eager to improve Liberia's future. It seems the Ebola crisis in Liberia was so severe, and the potential implications for the world of such great magnitude, it placed a much-needed world spotlight on Liberia just as Katie's work was beginning to shine.

Yet even Katie, the woman who walked into the center of a killer epidemic, into the heart of a dying slum, and into the hearts of the Liberian people, occasionally feels fear.

"I have always been very bold. I always stood up for what I believed in. But at the same time, I was afraid. And I am still afraid. But a leader isn't someone who isn't afraid. A leader is someone who is afraid and acts anyway."

While success has come quickly, it has been an incredibly difficult journey. The days are long, the surroundings coarse, even before Ebola struck. Looking back, Katie considers much of the path to be a spiritual journey.

"More than Me is very spiritual for me. I don't talk about it often, because people aren't always open to that. I started off with Jesus being a big part of my life. As I traveled and met so many people, and enjoyed help from so many diverse people, like the Muslim woman from Lebanon I originally stayed with who covers herself head to toe, and the liberal churches, and my Pentecostal mother, and the people I've been able to share stories and meals and time with—I began to see the world through their eyes. Meeting polygamist Christians who are happy, thinking of my Jewish friend who helped me along the path—I reflect on all of these different people who made this happen. Sometimes I think that's as much of the point as the kids going to school.

"When you are trying to get a 9-year-old girl out of prostitution and into school, it doesn't matter what religion you follow, or anything you are or do. It doesn't matter what box you check on the census, you can agree that no 9-year-old girl deserves to be a prostitute. So all the different people of different backgrounds and faiths who came to the table to get this program started—and they don't always know they are at the same table—I see God in that. That's the point: getting past all these things that separate us, and coming together to see how can we work together in a way to make the world a better place."

SCOTLUND HAISLEY
Founder, Animal Rescue Corps

ENDING ANIMAL SUFFERING THROUGH DIRECT AND COMPASSIONATE ACTION

"I have to believe that we are all born with this gift of compassion, yet we live in a society that forces us to either ignore it, hide from it, or bury it. I have the ability to embrace my own compassion, and rather than see it as a weakness as most men do, I see it as one of my greatest strengths."

In the heat of summer, one day before Independence Day, 2014, Scotlund Haisley and his team at Animal Rescue Corps launch *Operation Liberty Dogs* in Page County, Virginia. The target is a massive, backwoods breeding enterprise known in the rescue world as a puppy mill. By 5 a.m., Scotlund's team is assembled; it includes the local sheriff's department, the Virginia state veterinarian, local rescue groups, and scores of local volunteers. The temperature and humidity are already oppressive at dawn.

The Sheriff's department leads the initial charge, securing the property and detaining the puppy mill operators. Next, the Animal Rescue Corps team arrives, Scotlund at the helm.

The situation they encounter can only be described as horrific. Puppies and their moms are living in deplorable conditions. Most of the dogs are filthy, some beyond recognition, with fur matted into painful twists that pull at the skin. Scotlund holds up a dog whose eye is literally matted shut, indicating months, if not years, of neglect. Another dog lies in his cage, life barely detectable. They find a weak heartbeat and rush him to a local emergency clinic where he will be given a life-saving blood transfusion. In all, emergency treatment will be needed to save six dogs that had been left to die alone in their cage, and countless others will require at least some medical attention.

Animal Rescue Corps
Photo by Kristina Bowman

A typical puppy mill hidden by surrounding forest.

Twelve long, hot, and trying hours later, the rescue continues. "We've got nothing to complain about," Scotlund says. "These dogs have been living in these unbearable conditions their entire existence. We are not leaving until 100% of these dogs are off the property."

As more and more puppies and dogs are lifted from rusted, feces-laden metal cages, they are triaged by a volunteer veterinarian before being sent to a makeshift clinic for treatment.

Animal Rescue Corps
Photo by Kristina Bowman

Scotlund holds a severely matted puppy he's just rescued.

It's nearing darkness when the mission is finally complete. The face-masks, worn to protect volunteers from the stench and disease, have all been removed and the team moves from the putrid hellhole to the temporary shelter.

"It's been an amazing day and we are exhausted," Scotlund says. "We've removed 132 dogs and four birds from that property and they are resting here at our emergency shelter. We will be able to fulfill our commitment to these animals to get them into loving homes. For the first time, they will get to live their lives as dogs instead of prisoners, and live in a way they have never had the opportunity to do."

FINDING PURPOSE IN UNLIKELY PLACES

"I got clean when I was 20, and by the time I was 21, I was feeling like I could give back to the world. I'd already gone through the worst."

Scotlund's skill in precision planning and execution of major projects, his strong and poignant leadership, and his extensive knowledge of animal behavior are not the result of an advanced education. In fact, Scotlund never received formal education of any kind. His diverse skill-set, and likely his sense of compassion, was learned and earned throughout his difficult and lonely childhood lived out on the streets, where gang members and drug dealers were his teachers. It was gang members who taught him how to read, write, and survive.

Scotlund doesn't dwell on his childhood experiences, other than to say that his father was an abusive alcoholic whose behavior was so egregious that his mother escaped and took his siblings with her, leaving him to face life alone with his dad. It wasn't long before Scotlund felt it safer to escape—to anywhere—than remain at home. At the age of 11, he walked out his father's front door, never to return. He found a new family among local gangs and drug dealers, leading to a decade of hard drinking, drug addiction and homelessness. For nine long, hellish years, daily life was often a literal fight for survival.

"I got clean when I was 20, and by the time I was 21, I was feeling like I could give back to the world. I'd already gone through the worst. How could anything else be any worse? Oh my God, there's a huge freedom in that! I wouldn't wish my childhood on anyone, and I'll do everything in my power to make sure that my children don't experience that. But I'm damn grateful for it because it's made me who and what I am. It's given me hope and the strength to do what I do."

The parallels between Scotlund's own life and his career in saving the most vulnerable creatures are almost too obvious to mention. He doesn't shy away from the fact that his difficult past led to his current work.

Reflecting back, he remembers the first time he faced his own compassion, as it stood in stark contrast to the violent world in which he lived.

"I was 10 years old, and I shot a bird with a BB gun. I pointed my gun at a sparrow perched on a tree branch. I remember being surprised that I was allowed to do that, that I had that power. I pulled the trigger and shot it, and the sparrow fell to the ground and began bleeding. I remember thinking, 'What did I just do?' I connected to his pain and I felt horrible. I realized what I had done was the worst thing. My friend said, 'Now you have to put him out of his misery. You've got to pick him up and twist his head like a bottle cap.' I did that, and killed the bird. In that moment I understood compassion. I understood I didn't need to do what I had done."

RESCUING ANIMALS, DAY IN AND DAY OUT

"[It] perpetuates the stereotype that shelters are dark, dingy places where animals live in fear and loneliness until they are put to death."

When Scotlund was 21, he began his career in animal rescue. It started with a job as a Humane Officer for the Humane Society of the United States, often aiding police and animal control with removing animals from abusive situations. It was fulfilling work, but he quickly became frustrated with what happened once the animals were rescued and placed in a shelter.

"I immediately recognized the biggest problem we have is housing animals in cages. We put an animal alone in a cage, and they decline emotionally, socially and physically, almost upon entry.

"There are three stages of decline. First is high anxiety, the barking. The steel, barred cages cause what is termed, 'cage-rage.' They can see and hear what's on the other side, but they can't get to it and they become frustrated. Over the following days and weeks they go into the second stage—depression. They go to the back of the cage and they're not showing themselves as an animal in your home—no one would want to adopt them. The third phase is psychological turmoil, and then in a sense the animal is destroyed. I'm not saying the animal can't be brought back, but it certainly can't be brought back living in the environment that created it. That's our sheltering system. The goal is—or should be—to find these animals permanent loving homes. So we're shooting ourselves in the foot by putting these dogs and cats in an environment that works against them and not for them, and we're creating an environment that works against the public and perpetuates the stereotype that shelters are dark dingy places where animals live in fear and loneliness until they are put to death. We are ruining the product that we're trying to sell, and we're not selling them well either."

After his first job as a humane officer in Washington D.C, Scotlund held a series of increasingly-responsible local and international positions over the next twenty-three years, but his dissatisfaction with counterproductive shelter practices never left him. With each position he held, he would refine and redefine the way the animals were looked at and treated.

He moved to Ponce, Puerto Rico, to establish an animal shelter, train employees, and create a set of sheltering standards. Next, he was off to New York City, where he was hired to direct the NYC Shelter. The San Francisco Bay Area Humane Society then asked him to work as captain of Humane Law Enforcement, which led to a stint in India, where he worked with Maneka Ghandi, daughter-in-law of Indira Gandhi, establishing new standards in animal sheltering for India. Eventually, he returned to Washington, D.C., where he was made Captain of Humane Law Enforcement for the Washington Humane Society.

These twenty-three formative years in animal rescue gave tremendous purpose to Scotlund's life, and they honed his natural skill set. But perhaps more importantly, it nurtured his deep need to do something more creative, and reinforced his inexorable desire to fundamentally change the way we view and treat sheltered animals.

WASHINGTON ANIMAL RESCUE LEAGUE— TEAR IT DOWN

"I literally cried the day we first put dogs in those dens because this was all a huge gamble! In my heart I believed it would work, but when I saw the tangible outcome…it was just amazing."

The opportunity to make watershed change in animal shelters came in 2001 when Scotlund was invited to direct a no-kill shelter in Washington, D.C., a job he did not initially want to take. "They had a reputation for being well-funded due to their founding in 1914, but they were quite worthless to the community; they simply warehoused animals and had established no worthwhile programs. I didn't want the job at first, then the thought came to me: 'Maybe I could fix it!'

"It was at that shelter where I finally found my platform to create what I had to ultimately design and build, that which I had been looking to create all along. I just hadn't realized I'd been looking for it.

"I started with the staff, firing almost everyone. If an organization is not working, it's not working because it doesn't have leadership. When it hasn't had leadership, the people in place are used to functioning without it and they rarely respond when leaders do show up. A few individuals did respond immediately and I kept them around because I needed someone who could provide consistency, even though I was about to turn everything upside down.

"Immediately I began doing things that made people very nervous. I started creating new programs, new standards of care. Then I reached out into the community to meet their needs. I started a SHARE program, Shelter Animal Relief Effort, where we went into other shelters, locally, regionally, and beyond, taking any animal that was slated to be put to death, and bringing it back to our D.C. shelter.

"I initiated a 'Free Spay and Neuter' program, a key service that needed to be done in order to slow growth in the local animal population. I wanted to make it so nobody had any excuses not to spay or neuter their pet. We offered the service free to everyone, not just the low-income community. That created some tension between the board members because now I had people pulling up in Lexuses and getting free spays and neuters. But what they didn't realize was that that was the best thing that could happen— getting that rich person inside the building. I got their name, I got their mailing address, and I gave and received a positive experience. I knew they would ultimately provide far more than $100 the spay or neuter would have cost."

WASHINGTON ANIMAL RESCUE LEAGUE— REBUILDING FOR THE ANIMALS

"Well, dogs could give a shit about decorative tile. It's nicer for you, but it's not built from the dog's perspective or the cat's perspective."

At no point in the process did Scotlund let conventional wisdom or the status quo get in the way of making a difference. After establishing the new programs, hiring a great staff, and setting up high standards, he wanted to redesign the shelter to get the animals out of their cages and into an environment that encouraged people to visit the shelter. His goal was to set the animal and the adopter up for success. He knew in his heart that changing the game would require bold thinking, and he quite literally had to think outside the box.

"We were housing animals in this traditional, prison-like environment; central cellblock looking, standard chain-link fence cages. Our goal as a humane society was to find these animals permanent, happy homes. We were working against our mission when we housed them in an environment that breeds anxiety, frustration, depression, and aggression. So I knew we needed to create a cage-free environment, but we had hundreds of animals, 300 cats and 200 dogs, and you're not just going to let them all roam free."

The first step was to open cages and let dogs interact. "I did that on like, day two. The staff was blown away by it. They would tell me, 'Wait! That dog's aggressive!' And I told them, 'Well, he's not going to be now.' It just goes to show how little we understand animals."

After successfully pairing or grouping all the dogs, having proven his concept that dogs needed socialization and that all shelter pets needed to be living cage-free, he set out to hire an architect.

He knew a complete renovation was going to cost millions of dollars, that he would need to gut the place, and create a whole new environment. Rather than going to the board, he started feeding certain board members information because he wanted to gather support when it came time for a vote.

It's not only strategic planning skills that make Scotlund's tactics so successful; it's his intuitive understanding of how people—and animals for that matter—think.

"I was introducing some crazy thoughts that nobody had ever heard of or seen before, like installing water fountains running over dog tents. So I needed to have a solid argument before I walked into that boardroom. I needed to find an architect to help visualize what I had conceptualized. I wanted to make sure they had never set foot in an animal shelter before because all of the architects out there that are doing shelters are doing the same thing, like decorative tile on the dog dens. Well, dogs could give a shit about decorative tile. It's nicer for you, but it's not built from the dog's perspective or the cat's perspective."

As he describes it, Scotlund needed to convince 25 D.C. socialites who funded the shelter that a new, cage-free concept was the best thing that they could do, and he needed $15,000 to get started with an architect. He visited a sympathetic board member individually, and asked her, "Will you believe in me? In what's possible?" She said, "Absolutely," and gave him a $15,000 donation. With that he put together a 90-page proposal, complete with architectural renderings and pricing.

But Scotlund wasn't content with only creating a cage-free environment. He looked at every aspect of the animal's lives inside the shelter and found ways to improve each one. Knowing that animals benefit from sunlight, he insisted on installing skylights. To prevent cage-rage, they decided on placing translucent glass blocks between the dens. Heated floors were a must, as were murphy-style beds that could be flipped up if the dogs didn't use them. The list went on: self-filling water bowls to ensure a constant source of clean water, individual air exchanges to help prevent the spread of airborne illness, and guillotine style doors that allowed the dogs to defecate away from where they slept. Finally, a running water system was installed above the dens; one that the dogs could see and hear. Soothing harp music would play at all times.

"I was ready. I had done all of my research and knew what I wanted. I sent it to the board on a Friday before a scheduled board meeting the following Monday. I made the presentation, and within 10 minutes they said, 'This is going to cost us 4 million dollars, and it's obviously going to increase your operation, which means we need to increase our endowment fund.' Still, they were impressed, and after considerable discussion told me, 'If you can raise 6 million dollars, you can do this.' So they approved it, we raised the money, and we built it!

"In 2006 we opened the world's first cage-less animal shelter, the Washington Animal Rescue League. After we moved all the animals in, you could walk into a room of a hundred dogs and hear a pin drop. That's the first time I'd ever, ever witnessed such a thing. It all worked! I literally cried the day we first put dogs in those dens, because this was all a huge gamble! In my heart I believed it would work, but when I saw the tangible outcome… it was just amazing."

When the shelter opened, numerous national magazines and newspapers covered the story. "Everything changed. Adoptions went up over 400%. I was there one weekend and there was a man in the cat room, and I asked if he was there to adopt another pet, and he said, 'No, Scotlund, I come here every weekend to bring my children because this is a community center.'"

THE CRESCENDO—
LAUNCHING ANIMAL RESCUE CORPS

After four years as the Senior Director of Emergency Services, Scotlund made the most pivotal decision of his life.

With the new center open and unprecedented success under his belt, he received his next call to action. The CEO of the Humane Society of the United States called and said, "Scotlund, you've done great things here, but it's time to get you on the national front." He accepted the position of Senior Director of Emergency Services, and over the next four years built and led an international rescue team as well as a team to investigate puppy mills and dog fighting rings.

If there is a maxim that Scotlund fully embodies, it is this: "If you want something done right, do it yourself." The Humane Society of the United States is, after all, an enormous organization, founded more than 60 years ago, and with total assets exceeding a quarter-billion dollars. Their massive size and wealth allows them to undertake several projects simultaneously, but their monolithic stature and procedural bureaucracy can be a nightmare for someone of Scotlund's nature.

After four years as Senior Director of Emergency Services, Scotlund made the most pivotal decision of his life. In 2010, he left HSUS and formed the non-profit organization, Animal Rescue Corps, also known as ARC.

"I started ARC because I was looking for the gaps that needed to be addressed. There are so many groups doing so many different things. The bigger groups do 100 things and everything they do is at 50%. I wanted to create an organization that did a few things at 100%. It's these mid-level groups where you can be efficient and effective, and that's what I wanted."

Scotlund launched ARC with five people, himself included. Carla and Tim came with him from HSUS and were, in his estimation, absolutely essential to making a go of it. With passion and purpose aligned, they were focused and moving fast. Within one month of opening, Animal Rescue Corps conducted their first massive puppy mill rescue. Their work and impact has expanded exponentially since then.

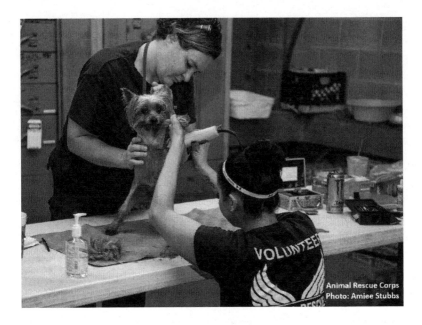

Post rescue, ARC Volunteers lovingly provide medical care and grooming for neglected or tortured animals.

ROUGHING IT

"What was important was to fulfill our mission right away, not to pay people or buy things, but to do the work and prove to people who we were."

Like many dedicated world changers, Scotlund has the ability and willingness to work exceedingly hard for little or no pay in order to make a real difference.

"For the first year we didn't pay ourselves anything, and it was a struggle. I had to absorb all of my retirement. I knew I was tired of working in a bureaucratic world because bureaucracy should play no role in animal protection, so I was willing to make the sacrifice. We all made sacrifices. Tim and Carla are my left and right hands and we all sacrificed together. I almost lost my house but a good friend and donor bailed me out. Still, I would have done this living in a cardboard box—there was no question about it."

Scotlund had real advantages after working in the field for twenty-three years before launching ARC. He had a track record, a reputation, and, he had contacts.

"What was important was to fulfill our mission right away, not to pay people or buy things, but to do the work and prove to people who we were. Our first rescue was a puppy mill in February in Tennessee. We went to the authorities, made the case, and I said let's go. I asked a well-known animal rights supporter if he would fund my first rescue, and he agreed."

UNDERCOVER OPERATIONS MEETS ANIMAL RESCUE

"We research everybody who will be involved, like asking if the sheriff goes to the same church as the bad guy. We know all of the players before we get there, and they don't even know we exist."

A rescue essentially unfolds like this: An individual or group discovers an abuse or neglect case involving a large number of animals. They contact Animal Rescue Corps to ask them to investigate. Scotlund and his team conduct a thorough investigation and, if they believe they can build a case on it, the person who provided the tip may become an informant. If that's the case, they send them a contract and the informant begins taking directions from ARC.

Regardless of whether they bring in their own people or bring in an informant, Scotlund and his team begin to build a case. They acquire undercover photos and videos. If they can get a veterinarian on the property to document the situation they will, and anything else they can do to build a strong case, they do. Once they've constructed a solid case, they create a report, usually 30-90 pages. Scotlund gets on a plane to the site, picks up the local informant or the investigator, and usually approaches the local authorities. This step takes some analyzing and finessing, and every case is unique.

"I need to decide who to approach. All this is done through web searching to see if the district attorney has had any success in prosecuting animal cruelty in the past. We research everybody who will be involved, like asking if the sheriff goes to the same church as the bad guy. We know all of the players before we get there, and they don't even know we exist."

Though Scotlund knows the case will ultimately end with the county attorney or the district attorney, he begins with the lowest level person with authority. "If I don't start there, then typically I am creating bad blood between myself and that person. Nobody likes to be told what to do, and they want to be the hero. My objective is to make them the hero.

"I go in and say, 'Here's the case, here's all the resources. We'll do everything, and all you have to do is get a warrant and take credit for it.'"

As enticing as that may sound, even that request can present a challenge.

A DANGEROUS EXECUTION

"I'm not afraid of anything, really. I've been shot, I've been stabbed, I spent many years as a child on the streets, I've overdosed, I've basically died many times. I've made it through all of that, so the worst has already happened."

"I'm a guy coming from Washington, D.C., into rural Kentucky. There's a level of distrust."

Fortunately, after so many years doing rescues, Scotlund has a solid list of district attorneys who will act as a reference. Still, it's always very dynamic and it's never a smooth process. There are multiple moving parts and Scotlund's job is to manage them all.

Poised to bust a rural dog fighting ring or a massive puppy mill, Scotlund knows he's messing with people's livelihoods, and that is a dangerous mission. Yet, despite the potential danger, he doesn't feel fear when they begin moving in with police to arrest the owners and rescue the animals.

"It's never about what I fear, it's never about me. I'm thinking about the responsibility I have as the one leading this rescue. I think about everybody, and I think of my family. I don't have pictures of my kids online; I keep my personal life as far from the organization as I can. I've had plenty of people threaten me. I'm not afraid of anything really. I've been shot, I've been stabbed, I spent many years as a child on the streets, I've overdosed, I've basically died many times. I've made it through all of that, so the worst has already happened. With that said, safety is a huge issue during these operations. As we are planning, I am looking out for everyone's safety. The volunteers understand it's dangerous work and they sign a waiver before they do anything."

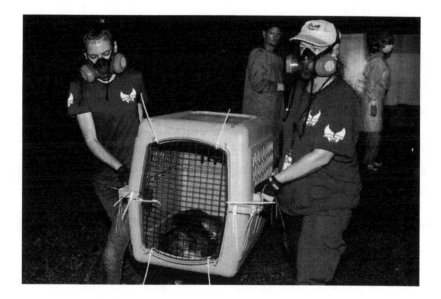

ARC employees removing a monkey from a Tennessee backyard.

THE PHILOSOPHY

"Of the places I have shut down, I've learned there is no such thing as a humane puppy mill, because it's always about mass production, and they are always in violation of the law."

Shutting down puppy mills is what ARC is best known for. Some question him on the absoluteness of this position, citing reputable breeders and a constant need for new puppies. His response is twofold, and it's important. Either by gas chamber, electrocution, or lethal injection, roughly two and a half million companion animals are euthanized in the United States alone each year. Supply far, far outweighs demand. If mass production can be stopped, eventually the immensely overcrowded shelters can downsize and return to a normal business of finding lost dogs and cats, caring for and adopting them out, and housing what might be considered a rational or normal amount compared to the massive population they currently serve. Today, more and more people demand specific breeds, and that leads to the killing of mixed or unwanted breeds to suit human preferences. It's the scale of production that causes the problem, not a family mating their pet with another to have a litter.

"If there's a family or an individual breeder who has a litter or two, and they sell those litters to individuals, that's not a problem. The minute the animal is no longer a family member and is a production machine, it becomes something else. So whether it's 10 or 1,000, it's a puppy mill. However, of the places I have shut down, there is no such thing as a humane puppy mill, because it's always about mass production, and they are always in violation of the law. The department of agriculture doesn't have the resources or manpower to regulate it, so they self regulate, and they often fudge their reports."

People argue that it doesn't make sense for mass breeders to harm the puppies or their mothers through neglect, because they can't sell an unhealthy animal. Surprisingly, that's not necessarily the case.

"If you hire a staff, that digs into your bottom line. The puppy mill owner only makes $50 a dog—it's the pet store making the real money. The puppies are often sold with diseases because of the environment or defects, but hopefully, from the puppy mill's perspective, they are sold before anybody can detect that. The unsuspecting buyer at the store purchases these puppies. They get them home, the pet gets sick, they spend thousand's of dollars to save them, and they also become victims."

BEYOND PUPPY MILLS

The rescue became front-page news nationally because the owner of the operation was a celebrated NFL player; Michael Vick, the number one draft pick in 2001.

Operation Liberty Dogs is one of countless rescue operations run by ARC since its inception in 2011. Others include *Operation Home for the Holidays, Operation Sweethearts, Operation Delta Dogs, Operation Forgotten Angels,* and many more. They haven't all been puppy mills. ARC addresses any large-scale cruelty of any animal in an industry that profits from their suffering. That includes factory farms, fur farms, hoarding, poorly run zoos, and dog fighting rings.

Operation Broken Chain was among the most horrific and heart-wrenching rescues the ARC team has conducted. The rescue became front-page news nationally because one of the owners of the operation was a celebrated NFL player; Michael Vick, the number one draft pick in 2001. As the federal judge would eventually state, Vick "promoted, funded, and facilitated a dog fighting ring on his property". That doesn't begin to describe the horror.

On Thanksgiving Day, 2012, local firefighters responded to a brush fire on Buckeye Road in Ashland City, Tennessee. What they found has been described as barbaric, brutal, and flat-out illegal. When firefighters entered the property to put out the flames, they found more than sixty pit bulls imprisoned by heavy chains. Buried car axles secured the chains—a common method used for securing fighting dogs because the pivoting axle prevents the chain from tangling. It turns out the dogs they found who were prevented from moving were the lucky ones.

Scotlund received the call for help, put together his team, and boarded a flight to Virginia within hours.

"You can never fully prepare yourself to witness the full extent and effects of cruelty and abuse. Even after more than 20 years fighting animal cruelty in all its forms, and having worked to free dogs from many dog fighting operations, I found myself very affected by the suffering these dogs and countless others on that property had to endure: their emaciated frames struggling to free themselves from heavy chains; the bones of other dogs littered on the ground in and around the old trash burn piles; their scars, untreated wounds, and broken bones; and the solitary noose hanging from one tree."

The noose, it turns out, was used to hang the dogs that lost fights. According to federal court transcripts. "The men tested the dogs in fights, then shot, electrocuted, or hung dogs who did not perform well. The fights usually occurred late at night or in the early morning, and would last several hours. Losing dogs sometimes died in the pit. Gambling purses were frequently in the thousands of dollars."

Scotlund and a volunteer use bolt cutters to free Michael Vick's fighting dogs.

Scotlund and his team took eleven of Vick's dogs to the same Washington, D.C., shelter Scotlund had reconstructed. "In the middle of the night, we separated half of the shelter. I assigned two caretakers solely to those suffering dogs, and we cared for them and brought them back to life. They were eleven of the most damaged dogs we ever took in. We had them for half a year, after which they went to Best Friends Sanctuary in Utah to live."

STRONG LEADERSHIP IS KEY

"My operation is specifically run like a military operation."

Regardless of scale, there are many key aspects that go into running any successful organization, but when both human and animal lives are at stake, everything must run like clockwork. Strong, clear leadership is the only way to ensure that it does.

"My operation is specifically run like a military operation. There is a chain of command. On every rescue I have a command chart, and I place volunteers in roles. Everybody who comes on board has to fit into that role and they have to abide by it, and if they don't, they're gone. I'm a hard ass when I'm out there; I'm a drill sergeant. People love it and they want it. They feel confident that their leader knows what he is talking about. I don't get questioned very often."

*Scotlund coordinating with local law enforcement on
a monkey and bird rescue operation.*

THE BIG PICTURE

"We film every rescue ourselves, which gives us the footage for education and training."

Scotlund is painfully aware that Animal Rescue Corps' operations treat only the symptoms of a vicious, profit-driven disease, and until public awareness reaches a tipping point that disease will continue to grow. Every time they rescue a single animal from a cruel situation, it's worth it, but the operations are costly, averaging between $25,000 and $75,000 each. Organizing the last-second volunteer manpower is no easy feat either.

"When we come into a town to shut down a property, we don't tell anyone, because we can't. Then, overnight we need 100 volunteers to show up from the town. I embrace the community through media. When we're on scene, I have the videographer and the photographer getting footage. They take a break half way into it, and we release a written press release so it's on the local news and sometimes the national news, depending on the case. That helps draw more volunteers."

Scotlund knows that there will never be enough money or enough volunteers to shut down every case of cruelty, but he is a big picture thinker, and he knows that in order for the public to care enough to do something, he needs to provide them with as powerful of a story as he can.

"I'm not telling you, I'm showing you. The stuff we are putting out there is unprecedented; nobody has had access to puppy mills, dog fights, and hoarding cases. We film every rescue ourselves, which gives us the footage for education and training. Naturally, it helps with fundraising as well. But our goal is to create a lasting solution. So we are training law enforcement people, giving them equipment and tools, establishing local humane societies. We do our best to set them up for success."

Today, ARC offers a basic animal rescue course, but eventually Scotlund wants to start a training academy. "For education, we eventually want a program for kids. Right now our education work consists of showing people the issues. But we will grow. We're going to change the way people think."

A HERO?

"The problem with being considered a hero, or having a hero status, is that expectations are great and you are no longer seen as a human. When I show human qualities, I create disappointment. It creates a lot of pressure."

As any family of a first responder knows well, emergency responses supersede family time, holidays, birthday celebrations and life in general. This can put immense stress on family members and relationships. When the fire occurred at Michael Vick's dog fighting property, it didn't matter that it was Thanksgiving Day. Scotlund's call to duty is absolute.

While days like that are difficult for the family, there are also upsides, like the swelling pride of watching your father be a badass on the nightly news. On both local and national news, Scotlund is often shown with bolt-cutters in hand, breaking the chains of abused and neglected animals. It makes him a bit of hero both at home and in communities across the country.

"My kids love what I am doing. They are so proud. They are always talking about their dad being on TV. I am a hero to them. But I know I'm not a hero. What I am is an individual who is dedicated to his work and very good at it. I recognized that this was my life's work at 22. However, I do recognize, right or wrong, in the minds of many, I am a hero. I understand the responsibility that goes along with that, being a role model. If people need heroes, great, I'm happy to be one. But I can only show one side of me, which is my work. The problem with being considered a hero, or having a hero status, is that expectations are great and you are no longer seen as a human. When I show human qualities, I create disappointment. It creates a lot of pressure. People come into this organization because of me, wanting to be close to me. It's an interesting phenomenon, and I recognize it.

"If I can inspire people to make decisions of positive change, for themselves and for animals, then I am all for it. The expectation of making me out to be something that I am not, that's a different thing altogether."

EMOTIONAL TOLL AND REWARDS

"I know the worst humanity has to offer, but I also know the best humanity has to offer."

For those who deal with desperately sad and discouraging situations where the odds against making a change are so disproportionate to the overall problem, one has to keep a solid core, maintain focus, and keep an inner balance. Sometimes it means postponing emotional feelings until a time and setting when they can be processed. But Scotlund believes they must get processed eventually.

"I learned how to maintain nothing but professionalism through these operations, and look at them through a legal perspective rather than an emotional perspective. The more professional and legally accurate I can be, the better off the animals are going to be.

Scotlund copes with his constant exposure to animal suffering by painting his emotions onto canvas, or in this case, tin ceiling tiles.

"As for my emotions, I can let them loose later, and I absolutely do. I fall apart. Sometimes it hits me in my hotel room, often when I'm painting. It's then I can connect to just that one animal, as opposed to during the operation. Imagine the tremendous responsibility and pressure on me during the operation: I've convinced the local authorities that they need to take this place down. I have the responsibility to make everything go as planned, otherwise it's my fault and I've failed. I accept the responsibility and any fault. I can do that because I've suffered. It's a gift because I can empathize with that level of suffering. My life goal is to end as much suffering as I can before I die and inspire others to carry on."

"I know the worst humanity has to offer but I also know the best humanity has to offer. In my work, I feel that I get to equalize it."

PAUL POLAK

Founder, Windhorse International &
International Development Enterprises

REVOLUTIONIZING DESIGN TO SERVE
THE WORLD'S POOREST PEOPLE

"If you are doing this with charity, there is never going to be enough money in the world to give people access to safe drinking water who don't have it, or to provide electricity. But if you make it a self-sufficient business there is no limit to scale as far as access to capital."

Paul Polak has helped millions of people move out of poverty, yet he doesn't necessarily think of his work as 'doing good.' He just likes to get things done.

"Did I have an inspiration with a ray of light from the heavens? No. I followed my nose and took advantage of the events as they unfolded. I am an entrepreneur and a contrarian, and whatever is impossible to do, that holds great attractiveness for me."

After more than eight decades, the one *impossible* feat that continues to hold the greatest attractiveness for Paul Polak is crushing global poverty. His incredible success in doing so has been a godsend for tens of millions of people whose lives have been uplifted across Asia, Africa, and Latin America.

Eschewing charity as a poverty trap, he instead creates income and livelihood opportunities for the most impoverished individuals on the planet. His method is consistently straight forward—identify the most pervasive problem and find the least expensive, longest-term solution. His projects have had tremendous range, from re-engineering donkey-carts for Somalian farmers, to rethinking simple irrigation techniques the world over, to proving to the world's largest, multinational corporations that marketing products to the 2.7 billion people living on less than $2 a day can be an economically sound strategy.

Global poverty numbers are so staggering they can knock the air from you when you first hear them. Like a man in a hurry to get back to work, Paul Polak sums them up quickly: "The numbers are nutty. There are 7.3 billion people on this planet, 90 percent of whom can't afford basic products and services. Nearly three billion people don't have regular access to food, shelter or clean water."

This situation does not sit well with him, and is the reason he has spent the last 30 years of his life doing, quite literally, everything in his power to change it. He shows no signs of slowing down either; on the contrary, he works eighty hours a week to change as much as he can, as fast as he can, while he can.

The beauty of it all is the way he easily smiles and jokes his way through most days as if engaged in the most satisfying work a person can do.

A TROUBLING BEGINNING

"He was a survivor because he was able to see and react sooner than most people."

Born to a Jewish family in Czechoslovakia in 1934, Paul Polak was just five years old when the Holocaust began. Despite the horror of that time, he attributes much of his success in helping the poorest of the poor to that early experience and the lessons he learned.

"In 1939, Jewish refugees began streaming across the [German] border with broken heads, in great numbers, so it was very clear to anybody willing to open their eyes that it was time to get out of there. Still, my dad could hardly get anyone to leave. He always saw the obvious, and I think I absorbed some of that capacity. He was a survivor because he was able to see and react sooner than most people. Eventually many people agreed, 'It's time to get out of here,' but it was too late. So that's one—I tend see the obvious.

"Two, being an entrepreneur and a problem solver is in my blood. My dad came from a peasant farm in which the animals lived downstairs and the family slept upstairs. I visited that farm as an adult, and I think I have a feeling for that. It gives me a sense of kinship with poor farmers."

When Paul was six years of age, his immediate family made the move that his extended family would not. Leaving their home and family in Czechoslovakia, they moved to the entirely foreign, but decidedly more secure, Canadian countryside. Using the bulk of the money they'd been able to scrabble together before fleeing, his father was able to purchase a small farm where he and his wife raised Paul and his brother in safety and peace. Several years later and after the war ended, Paul took a trip back to Europe to revisit the home he'd left as a child.

"My grandmother was gassed in Auschwitz. When I was a teenager, I took some time to visit the places where my grandmother lived during the time. I went to see a transit camp in Czechoslovakia, and later on, I took my own kids there. I was very aware of the hatred."

Despite his Jewish heritage and his lifelong marriage to Aggie, a Mennonite Minister, Paul is not a religious man.

"I'm not a church-goer," he states definitively. "My father used to go to a Catholic cathedral when he was younger because there were no synagogues where we lived in Canada. I asked him how he did that, and he said, 'Well it's all one God, isn't it?'

"So, I'm not religious. But for me, there is a spiritual thing about being a part of something bigger than myself, and that sense of connectedness is very central in my life. And with my family history...when we passed the milestone of helping 6 million, dollar a day, 1-acre farmers, it held great meaning for me."

Paul Polak testing new irrigation techniques alongside farmers in their crop fields.

Although it was not religion or spiritual leaders who inspired Paul Polak, his spiritual belief that we are all connected defines his life purpose; it is, in fact, his *raison d'etre.*

The surprise of Paul Polak, and perhaps another reason for his success, is the co-mingling of two very different sides of his personality: one, a no-nonsense, hard-charging, *get your hands dirty* work ethic; and two, his seemingly infinite compassion and empathy for nearly everyone on the planet. Despite his concern for the human condition and his respect for the health of the planet—which always figure boldly into his solutions—he often speaks more like a person managing a construction project, resolving complex logistical challenges while seeking better, faster, and cheaper ways to make change happen.

To get to the deeper side of what inspires this man to do what he does, it may be more revealing to read the poetry he occasionally feels compelled to write. It seems the surest way to reveal the territory that lies within.

A Deeper River

I have in me a deeper river
That flows toward the light
It does not ask me where to flow
It flows
And I flow with it
And then the river becomes the light
And we are one

MAKING SIMPLE WHAT EVERYONE ELSE COMPLICATES

The link he discovered between mental illness and poverty piqued his curiosity about how poverty impacts lives across the world.

Paul Polak's awareness that he wanted to improve the standard of living for the poorest people of the world germinated in an unlikely place—a psychiatric hospital. Before he took on the issue of poverty at the age of fifty, he worked as a psychiatrist for twenty-three years.

Even then he was an entrepreneur who challenged the system, always seeking innovative ways to help patients make significant strides in their recovery and coping mechanisms. He was one of the early leaders of the *de-institutional movement*, creating a system of private homes that replaced admission to psychiatric hospitals for acutely-psychotic patients.

"I started asking people why they were in the psychiatric ward at the hospital and their answers rarely matched that of their doctor. The patients often told me they were in mental health treatment because of a disturbance in their real-life setting, and 60% of the time that disturbance was a financial problem. Within that 60%, it was always a combination of the two factors: mental problems and poverty. So, I was working on practical solutions to help people with mental illness. It was never enough to interview people in my office."

Paul's connection was always with the person, not the disease. He looked beyond the confines of hard psychiatry to seek simple, human-based treatment, a pattern he would later extend to impoverished farmers.

"I developed an approach called *social systems intervention*, which trained mental health professionals to look beyond the symptoms of mental illness to the social disturbances in real life, which always included a lot of family issues, and beyond that, into the environmental context. If you look at the chronically mentally ill living in the community, things like housing, jobs, and self esteem are very strong predictors of re-admission to the hospital."

The link he discovered between mental illness and poverty piqued his curiosity about how poverty impacts lives across the world. A mentally ill patient in a typical American community may live on as little as $600 a month. In Bangladesh, most people live on less than $30 a month.

"I got curious about the social system to which a person belonged, and the environmental impact of that system, of which poverty played an important role."

THE SHIFT FROM PSYCHIATRY
TO POVERTY REDUCTION

*"That small effort got me directly involved in working in developing countries
with desperately poor populations. I became deeply inspired."*

While his thoughts were percolating about the effects of poverty on mental
health, Paul found himself in a situation that would effectively shift his life's
work from ruminating about reducing poverty to tackling it head on.

"I'm a scuba diver, and I set up a dive shop in Belize in the early days with
my diving buddy, Harry. We hired the local lighthouse keeper, a fisherman named Willard, to run our shop. Harry happened to be a commercial
fisherman, so together we came up with ways Willard could improve his
fishing success and raise his income."

It was 1964, and Paul's actions to help Willard make more money doing
what he was already doing, fishing, was the pivotal connection between
thinking about poverty and taking action to change it. Willard didn't need
a different way to make a living, he just needed to become more efficient at
what he was already doing.

"That small effort got me directly involved in working in developing countries with desperately poor populations. I became deeply inspired and
decided I would write a concept paper about creating a multinational corporation to help spur development in poor regions."

Paul's wife, Aggie, who was studying in a Mennonite seminary at the time,
had befriended the peace theologian John Howard Yoder. She connected
Paul and Yoder, who ended up writing the concept paper. Yoder gathered
together businessmen who were also interested in development, most of
whom, like Aggie, were Mennonites.

The result was the launch of International Development Enterprises, now
known as IDE—an immensely successful non-profit organization that just
celebrated its 30-year anniversary. With a $20 million budget and nearly

500 employees working hands-on in the poorest nations of the world, their impact continues to be enormous and far-reaching.

IN TECHNOLOGY, SIMPLICITY IS
THE ULTIMATE SOPHISTICATION

"What do I know about irrigation?" he adds, chuckling. "I was trained in psychiatry."

Polak's concept for IDE was to find and employ the simplest, easiest answers to empower people to make more money, and after more than 30 years, the organization remains true to that philosophy.

The products IDE designs and improves upon are not sexy by Western standards. On the contrary, some could be considered nearly primitive. Nevertheless, they are extremely effective, enough to lift families out of subsistence levels into more healthful and satisfying lives.

When Paul began investigating the lifestyles and environment of people living in poverty in undeveloped countries, the statistic that really stood out to him was this: 70 percent of the world's 2 billion poorest people live in rural areas and survive by growing crops on small plots of land. That information helped guide his first effort to find and distribute low-cost, low-tech tools that would assist this massive number of people to grow and distribute more crops in an earth-friendly way. In practical terms, that meant teaching individuals to build and sell simple and radically affordable products that help them make money, and by teaching others to buy and use those tools.

He began with the most basic tool still used today—donkey carts. While visiting a refugee camp in Somalia in 1982, Paul noted that a mere lack of transport kept the refugees from trading and getting supplies. At the time, some Somalians were using simple, but ineffective, donkey carts. In keeping with his vision of utilizing simple, low–cost technology, IDE re-engineered the cart to become far more efficient and capable of carrying large loads. He worked with local artisans to build and sell the carts.

Locals eventually produced and sold 500 carts, resulting in $1 million in net income for the cart owners. The solution was simple and effective; for the people of Somalia—it was dramatically life changing.

In 1984, he formalized IDE into a formal non-profit organization. He focused first on the desperately poor country of Bangladesh. As Paul listened closely to poor farmers while they worked in their fields, he learned their greatest problem was a lack of access to water for irrigating their crop fields. They had rain, but used only buckets to gather, store, and distribute it when they needed to irrigate their crops.

He began searching for a better tool, and discovered a human-powered treadle pump that had just been invented. The device is simple: a suction pump is perched on top of a well, and as the farmer begins to move his or her arms and legs in a rhythmic manner, it draws water up from the well less than twenty feet below the surface.

A Bangladeshi mother operates a treadle pump
to water her family's rice field.

The beauty of the treadle pump is its simplicity and its low cost—between $20 and $100, including installation. Better still, because it is human powered, it requires no fossil fuel. The benefits are enormous: the farmers get water to increase the number and quality of their crops, and there is no cost for fuel or electricity. By using the pump, farmers can expand their crop production by one or two seasons, which significantly increases their income.

Although they identified a great solution for the farmers, it was only the first of many steps, with many more challenges to overcome. The greatest of these were production, education, distribution, and finance. Paul rolled up his sleeves and put his energy into making it all work. It was a massive endeavor.

One by one, Paul convinced 75 small manufacturing plants in Bangladesh to begin making treadle pumps. He and his team taught these small shop owners who may have been making bed springs, bicycles, or any number of random items, how to make the pumps. The next step was recruiting dealers to sell treadle pumps. They found 3000 village dealers to sell them at a 15% margin. Finally, they trained 2500 well drillers to install them. Village mechanics drilled the wells, installed the pumps properly, and then became marketing agents.

Paul explains that threshold volume is the critical piece that makes any business work. They had to sell enough pumps to make it viable.

"In order to do that, we spent most of our time learning to do village marketing. We created a full-blown marketing initiative, including a Bollywood film. We had to do that to reach volume. If you had a dealer in a village in Bangladesh, he was selling several things. In order to make it worth his while for the dealer to sell treadle pumps, he and his family had to sell 20 pumps, and the manufacturer had to sell probably 200, and the well driller also had to do enough volume.

"There were already hundreds of workshops and dealers—we just harnessed them and organized them." Chuckling, he adds, "What do I know about irrigation? I was trained in psychiatry."

By 2014, more than 1.5 million treadle pumps had been sold in Bangladesh alone. The introduction, marketing and distribution of those pumps resulted in $1.4 billion dollars in net additional income for the farmers per year—a huge accomplishment that moved farmers from living in abject poverty to living a life of greater stability and dignity.

Naturally, he didn't stop with Bangladesh. Since it began, IDE has sold 2 ½ million treadle pumps in eleven countries, and they make eight different versions for diverse areas, including saltwater options.

Today, IDE also provides farmers access to an array of farming tools, including a simple form of drip irrigation that reduces water consumption by 30-70 percent. This has allowed people in Zimbabwe to augment their diets with fresh vegetables, greatly helping the large population struggling with HIV/AIDS. IDE's simple drip irrigation products also helps coffee-bean farmers in Nicaragua by reducing the flowering time of plants from three years to one-and-a-half years. Again, the boost in income has been life giving.

In India and Nepal, where vast numbers survive on local gardens and small plots, 50,000 small-scale IDE drip irrigation systems have been purchased and installed, dramatically increasing the consumption of vegetables.

Occasionally IDE engages in one specific operation that is not replicated, as in Vietnam, where IDE opened a coconut processing plant and later transferred ownership and management of the plant to local business people who employ 80 workers and process $300,000 worth of coconuts grown by local farmers.

UPPING THE ANTE

His goal was to end global poverty, and all the non-profits in the world weren't going to be able to accomplish that task. It was time for a new approach, and he was going to need a bigger boat.

Even as IDE continues to help 20 million people work their way out of poverty in 13 countries as diverse as Nicaragua, India, Myanmar, Nepal, Vietnam, and Zimbabwe, Paul Polak knew there was much more to be done. While his work in the non-profit sector had produced remarkable results, a sobering clarity began to settle in as he looked back on his work. His goal was to end global poverty, and all the non-profits in the world weren't going to be able to accomplish that task. It was time for a new approach, and he was going to need a bigger boat.

Riding on the waves of irony, his "bigger boat" would be the boogeyman of poverty: Big Business. He believed that only by leveraging the massive financial reach, infrastructure, and capability of multinational corporations, sustained over time by their continuous need for profits as well as their ongoing ability to raise capital, could the world have hope of truly ending intractable poverty while also providing radically affordable, desperately needed goods and services.

As Paul bluntly stated in a TED talk back in 2011:

> *"Our approaches to development have failed. Corporate social responsibility is cosmetic. Charity doesn't help people move out of poverty. And impact investing is confused about social impact vs. profitability."*

So, while IDE continued working to reduce poverty levels, Paul changed his own focus to inspiring multinational corporations to make and market products for the largely untapped emerging markets of developing countries. He theorized that the unintended benefits of those efforts would serve to lift the global poor out of the abyss and would improve their quality of life by offering them products they could actually afford.

When Paul launched IDE thirty years ago, nobody believed that a market-based approach to eradicating poverty was possible. As he describes it, people felt that businesses were the oppressors that aided poverty. The consensus was that the last thing you would do is use business to end poverty. However, when they sold one million treadle pumps, it changed the whole field because people saw it was possible.

"Business by itself is simply a structure, neither good nor bad, but rather a matter of how one harnesses it. What I learned at IDE is that it's critical to reach scale, which is the biggest unsolved portion of development. The only way to reach scale is with big business.

"If you are doing this with charity, there is never going to be enough money in the world to give people access to safe drinking water who don't have it, or to provide electricity. But if you make it a self-sufficient business, there is no limit to scale as far as access to capital."

PROVIDING THE PROOF

He doesn't call on large corporations to be altruistic, just smart.

Despite his best efforts to convince multinational companies of his ideas to make products for those living under $2 a day, they weren't jumping onboard. In order to get them to act, Paul knew he'd have to prove the idea could be profitable.

Multinationals have a long history of excluding the poorest 90% of the world from their target markets. After all, the richest 10% of consumers are the ones with sufficient money to purchase and use their products. Most of the ubiquitous global companies don't market any of their products to the poorest billions living on less than $2 a day. Seemingly, selling to the richest 10% has been enough to sustain desired profits. And selling to the rural poor in their unreachable villages, in countries with poor infrastructure, is a task most multinational corporations eschew.

Citing the life-changing work of the Bill & Melinda Gates Foundation in health-related charities world wide, Paul Polak questions why Microsoft does not make any products for the nearly 3 billion people who live on less than $2 day.

"They could design and make products that would be game changers for an unconnected population."

He doesn't call on large corporations to be altruistic, just smart. Eventually someone is going to serve those markets by investing now in product development that will pay off for decades to come. He takes a two-pronged, carrot and stick approach to win them over.

He entices corporations with the gloss of billions of new customers and new profit streams, and also warns them that they ignore these markets at their own peril as their competitors will eventually beat them to it. He doesn't sugarcoat the process either, nor under-estimate the difficulty in radically refitting their business plans.

In his TED talk, he explained:

> "...[Multi-national corporations must] react quickly and effectively to learn how to operate successfully in emerging markets. But this will require nothing less than a revolution in how they currently design, price, and distribute their products. I'm going to spend the rest of my life trying to foment that revolution."

That is precisely what he has done and continues to do at breakneck speed. He began by writing a book to outline the strategy, titled: *The Business Solution to Poverty: Designing Products and Services for Three Billion New Customers.*

At the age of 76, he made the decision to step down from his position at IDE, and invest his retirement savings into launching three new companies: Spring Health, to provide clean, affordable drinking water; *Affordable Village Solar,* to provide solar-powered irrigation to small farmers; and *Transform Energy,* to provide clean, cheap energy.

Spring Health now sells clean drinking water to 146,000, $1 income-a-day customers in India, where 350 million out of 500 million people live in rural villages, and they are just beginning to ramp up. Of the 1 plus billion people drinking bad water that makes them sick, the great majority live in similarly remote villages. Difficulty in reaching these villages is the primary hurdle that stops big business.

"You do that by unleashing *last-mile distribution*. That's a term from the electrification movement. The last mile of providing electricity is the most expensive. Only in this case it's the last 500 feet."

Paul solved that 'last 500 feet distribution' problem by using the most creative and inexpensive methods possible to clean and deliver affordable water. Utilizing existing mom and pop shops that exist in nearly all villages, *Spring Water* builds a cement tank at their store. The shopkeeper fills the tank with available water that is always fecal contaminated. Local village staff travels around on motorcycles carrying a water purifier that runs electricity through a 5% solution of salt water to purify the water. The shopkeeper then sells the clean water at affordable prices, and makes a profit. For the remaining people who aren't close enough to the village to pick up clean water, they set up a cheap and efficient home delivery system.

"Consistent, reliable delivery every day is a critical factor in retaining customers, so we've rapidly expanded water delivery to homes by using auto rickshaws."

The beauty in all of this is that those who have been suffering and dying from the lack of clean water are now able to afford access to clean water. Paul's company is showing a profit, and multinational corporations are paying attention.

"Our goal is to create a new market, and to provide safe drinking water. We want to prove this is a market businesses should look to. We borrowed $2 ½ million for the business. In the 4th year we will have paid everything back and have generated $2 million in profit. In the 5th year, that jumps to $5 million in profits, and then goes up exponentially."

Still, it was difficult to find investors. "They tell me I have a good track record in the non-profit world but not in for-profit. They say my goals for scale are unheard of, and unlikely to be feasible. Blah, blah, blah."

Spring Health has already proven his point, but Paul likes to drive his point home. *Village Solar,* the second of the three companies, has installed eleven beta test systems so far on one-acre farms in India and they are working flawlessly. The solar panels generate enough electricity to irrigate 2 ½ acres of high-value crops even in the dry season. During the test run alone the average farmer increased net income by $1100-$2000.

His third company, *Transform Energy*, seeks to replace the use of coal with a biomass substitute. Paul has a volunteer team at Ball Aerospace working feverishly to make an affordable energy option for the $2 day customer.

"I gave them the challenge of designing a low-cost, village torrefaction kiln capable of producing enough briquettes to support a small industry such as a textile factory. Not surprisingly, we've faced many challenges, but the most recent samples that came out of the first prototype have been surprisingly good with caloric values comparable to coal."

Since China now gets 90% of its energy from coal, and India about 70%, the reduction of 15% of carbon emission by using agricultural waste would have a transformative impact on the 2 billion people living on $2 day and would make a significant impact on the environment.

With a proof of concept now firmly in place, Paul and his team are looking for new products to sell to end users, taking advantage of the motorbikes and the entire distribution system serving the villages.

"We are looking at nutritious soda pop for 5¢. It has bubbles, it has flavor, and it has all the vitamins a 13-yr old child needs. We will supply a packet of powder and the consumer can buy and add water and have a nutritious, bubbly drink. We are also working on a commercial form of *Plumpy'nut*, the high-nutrient, peanut butter-like substance given to starving babies in Africa that has restored life to those suffering from severe malnutrition.

LOVE WHAT YOU'RE DOING OR DON'T DO IT

"I do this because it's fun. And yeah, obviously it is important. I love the creativity, the problem solving…but I am picking those things that make a difference to the planet."

Paul Polak considers how to describe his driving force. "I don't mention passion because it's so built in its not even worth mentioning. If you are not highly motivated—I mean—you have to be willing to chew through cement to make these things happen. The problems we've encountered in getting our water business to the point where it is scalable are just unbelievable."

With his simple yet revolutionary ideas for eradicating poverty and getting clean water and needed products to the poorest people in the world, Paul Polak is a living legacy. While he scoffs at the use of any superlatives, he can't deny his enormous influence on the next generation.

"It is true I've had a big influence on the whole field. When I gave a talk a couple years ago in San Francisco, I was brought in as a sort of historical icon who helped create this field of design for the poorest 99%. But then I started talking about the future and they realized I wasn't dead yet."

Though his wry sense of humor and mischievous smile make it all seem easy, it's been a long, tough road.

Back at the beginning, it would take a full seven years before Paul was able to take a salary from IDE. He managed to provide for his family by creating and running side businesses until the non-profit was stable enough to pay him a full-time wage.

Even today, at the age of 82, he struggles financially because he continues to take risks to make a difference. That's a choice he's made.

"Right now I am living on my retirement fund, which isn't fair to put Aggie through. So, it's not the best thing financially. I have put my money and my life into forming these companies.

"But I'm not worried about it. In terms of my joy in life and the peace that I feel, nothing compares with it. I love solving problems and the creative process. Life is a work of art and so I just love it. I mean it's a pain in the ass, you know. I complain all the time. You know what it takes to start and run something. You have to pay attention to a lot of details.

"I do this because it's fun. And yeah, obviously it is important. I love the creativity, the problem solving; but I am picking those things that make a difference to the planet."

In recent years, he has been lauded for his work the world over. Considered a pioneer in many fields, he stresses the point that one should never do it for the accolades or the glory.

"You better not depend on that!" he says, laughing. "You've got to be willing and able to be on your own for an indefinite period of time with nobody helping. You'd better be doing this for yourself.

"Life is so..." Suddenly at a loss for words, he turns to his poetry, which reveals his deeper motivation, his spiritual actualization.

The Instrument

I am a receptacle, a messenger, an instrument

Bereft of choice and filled with power
I cry out but I am powerless
Led by the hand to an uncertain fate

It is
There is no point in arguing
It is

It comes with silence and an end of questions
And then I know
I am connected and I know
Where does it come from?
I do not know
Without remorse

It moves to others
Fills them up to overflowing
With perpetual incandescent light

We are laid bare
And filled with wonder
And our naked helplessness
Will change the world forever

LEAVING A LEGACY

Paul Polak's oft-quoted statement, *We need a revolution in design for the other 90%,* inspired a movement in engineering schools. The renowned Cooper Hewitt Smithsonian Design Museum created a traveling exhibit called "Design for the other 90%," which inspired engineering students across the country and globally. Universities and companies seek his counsel and expertise, and he's helped create courses at Stanford, MIT, Cal Tech, Santa Clara, and elsewhere to provide students with skills and motivation to engineer for the un-served 90% of people in the world.

Yet the man remains humble and unimpressed with the countless awards and honorary degrees he has received. "I would rather have a real impact," he offers, smiling, knowing full well just how significant that impact has been.

"I was always in left field when I started. And now I'm a bit out in left field again with this multinational movement, but there a lot of people ready to jump on the bandwagon."

Paul Polak's love affair with eradicating poverty keeps him energized and engaged. Now, in his 9th decade of life, he works non-stop, crisscrossing the globe from India, to South Korea, to Viet Nam and beyond, speaking, working, engaging, and experimenting—always experimenting.

Though he has no plans to stop working or even slow down, he does have his eye out for a successor, a task that could prove to be his greatest challenge yet.

LOUIE PSIHOYOS
Founder, Oceanic Preservation Society

EXPOSING COMPLEX ENVIRONMENTAL ISSUES AND PROMOTING ADVOCACY

"This generation that's alive right now is determining the fate not only of humanity, but the fate of millions of species for eternity. I don't get despondent over that, I get empowered. If we don't fix it, then who the hell is going to fix it?"

Imagine for a moment that you have verifiable, scientifically proven information about an unfolding situation that is destroying half the species on the planet, and if left unchecked, the very earth as we know it. Imagine further that political and business leaders the world over hold the same knowledge, yet will not take action to stop it either because it could impact their economies or cut into their profit margins. You understand it is up to your generation—not your children's generation, but your generation alone—to prevent and reverse the destruction, because if you fail to act now, it will simply be too late. Finally, imagine you possess the skills, knowledge, experience, and courage to educate the world's population and inspire them to change course and prevent further destruction. You will need to devote every bit of energy, money, effort, and years of life you have left in the hope it will be enough. You must risk standing up to big government, big oil, big business, powerful politicians, self-serving lobbyists, and astonishing corruption and apathy. Would you take on that challenge?

Louie Psihoyos chose to do exactly that, with no halfway measures. He is out to expose complex, global environmental issues and advocate sustainability through the use of film, photography, social media and collaboration. He founded the Oceanic Preservation Society, OPS, to serve as the catalyst.

While "Oceanic Preservation Society" may not sound revolutionary, consider that OPS is a double-entendre for special operations—military-speak for a small number of undercover, highly-trained individuals who carry out secret missions on unsuspecting targets. This is precisely what OPS does. Their mission statement is as strong as it is succinct: *Expose the Truth. Protect the Planet.*

Logic may dictate that protecting the health of our oceans would not, and certainly should not, necessitate covert operations; so the question is, who or what are we saving the oceans from? And why did this National Geographic photographer abandon his successful and enviable career to devote his life to the OPS mission? What urgency is driving him to take out all the stops—projecting his message on movie screens in over 220 nations, and on the face of such iconic buildings as the Empire State Building, the United Nations Building, and St. Peter's Basilica in Rome—in order to get the word out as quickly and broadly as humanly possible? Why are he and his team employing the latest in undercover technologies, including hidden microphones, buttonhole cameras, and James Bond-inspired stealth vehicles?

The answers to those questions are best revealed by following the trajectory of Louie Psihoyos's career, by examining the current threats our planet is facing, and by peering inside the worlds of science, politics, business, and the illegal sale of endangered species.

FROM NATIONAL GEOGRAPHIC PHOTOGRAPHER TO ACTIVIST FOR CHANGE

"We could lose half or more of all species by the end of the next century. Humanity is like an asteroid to the planet."

From the time National Geographic hired him at the age of twenty-three, Louie Psihoyos wanted his photographs to make a difference in the world. He was the first photojournalist hired in a decade by the highly-revered magazine, an action that reflected their appreciation not only for his ability to compose a great photo, but also for his technical skills, his intellect, and his deeply-held values.

"I came from the school of what you might call a *concern* photographer, in that if you could show man's inhumanity to man, you could influence change."

Louie proved he could affect change with a story he proposed and shot for the magazine in 1983. Influenced by an earlier story he had photographed on the incredibly high value of the things we discard into landfills—such as materials we first mine and later consider garbage—he was inspired to investigate recycling, an experiment being piloted in only two cities in the United States. That particular National Geographic issue about the value and promise of recycling reached 44 million highly-educated readers.

Letting people know what was possible with recycling at a time when most Americans were completely unaware had a significant impact on him. He came to fully understand how he could use his photographic skills to inspire action on a massive scale.

During his seventeen years with the magazine, he shot four stories about animal extinction, and for nearly a decade his career centered on stories about paleontology. Paleontology is the study of the history of life on earth based on what fossils reveal. It tells us about the role and place of humans and of ecologies of the past. That long view of our planet's history can and often does reveal the future, and in this case, reveals a very disturbing trend of a growing mass extinction.

"A lot of my friends work in paleontology, and I've been on dinosaur digs all over the world. I have witnessed the frustration of scientists who have been warning us for years that we must stop putting carbon into the air if we are to prevent another mass extinction."

The problem is, no one listens to scientists.

Inevitably, Louie made the connection between the mass extinction of the dinosaurs he was photographing and the global destruction that is threatening so many of our most beloved creatures today.

"You begin to think, 'That was so long ago,' but a similar mass extinction is going on right now."

So, how bad is the situation today? How significant is our human impact on the planet in terms of extinction? Looking only at oceans for the moment, consider that a full *ninety-percent of all large fish are already gone from the sea.* That is an astonishing number, yet even today few people are aware of it. When we do hear it, it can be difficult to embrace and comprehend the enormity of it, and many resist letting it in.

A troubling realization for Louie was that only a tiny number of individuals truly understand the gravity of a mass extinction and most do not realize that we are currently in the midst of one. Many of our planet's most beautiful creatures are disappearing at this moment and will never return. That list includes everything from tiny birds in the Amazon to the strongest and most awe-inspiring mammals we have come to love. African lions are on the absolute edge of extinction, down 90% in the past few decades; every species of tiger on earth is teetering on the edge; and even elephants, the ubiquitous symbol of strength and endurance, are all but gone. With 100 elephants being poached daily for their ivory, their extinction could happen as soon as 2020.

There are several factors driving this unprecedented destruction and they are all related to human activity: wide-scale commercial fishing and hunting (both legal and illegal); shipping traffic, which is decimating the blue whale; rapid ongoing destruction of rainforests, and with them, thousands of natural habitats; and global warming, which is continually raising the temperature of our oceans. For river and sea mammals, there are added problems of dams and boat traffic, entanglement in discarded commercial fishing gear, an array of discarded plastics, spills from oil and gas development, and a host of other pollutants.

We are destroying habitats of thousands upon thousands of species. The entire eco-system is in peril, including our own.

WHY FOCUS ON THE OCEANS?

"We are going to lose all the coral reefs by the middle of this century. There will only be remnants left."

With so much of our planet and its ecosystems under attack, why did Louie Psihoyos decide to focus his energy primarily on saving the oceans? Quite simply, because the oceans are essential for all life on the planet. While rainforests provide just over a quarter of the oxygen we breathe, marine plants provide two out of every three breaths we take.

Here is the point of urgency: scientists estimate that in the past forty years we have lost half the ocean's microscopic marine animals, or phytoplankton, and we continue to lose plankton at the rate of about 1% a year due to the warming of our oceans. We are putting tremendous amounts of carbon in the air, and an alarming amount of it is being absorbed by our oceans.

Louie explains the impact of that seemingly small one percent. "You start to think of the ramifications. About 70% of carbon is being absorbed by plants and trees, and 30% by the oceans. We used to think that was a good thing, but now we know that carbon is acidifying the oceans. When carbon dioxide reacts with water, it creates carbonic acid. When you start to acidify the oceans, everything with a carbon shell—like coral, shellfish, and some plankton—suffer dramatically. Almost all life in the ocean depends on creatures with a carbonic shell. Experiments have revealed that plankton and other carbon-shelled marine life are not able to grow their shells adequately, reducing their nutrition. That impacts all the fish in the food chain, including humans."

While it isn't easy to for humans to "see" changes in phytoplankton (millions of them fit into one drop of water), it is hard *not* to see the dramatic visual changes in coral reefs. It made worldwide news recently when scientists at James Cook University in Australia documented that 93% of the Great Barrier Reef is now 'bleached' to some degree, one-third of it severely. Reefs are bleaching from the warmer oceans, and the oceans are warming with the increasing frequency and intensity of El Nino events. While an El Nino is a natural climate phenomenon, climate scientists largely agree that the uptick in its occurrence and severity is due to human-induced climate change.

"I look at where we have been, where we are now, and where we are going. We are losing the oceans at an incredible clip —and not just the oceans, but all life on the planet. We are losing about 30,000 species a year! Species have always come and gone, but we are accelerating this rate to the point where we are facing a mass extinction...to the point that we could lose half or more of all species by the end of the next century. Humanity is like an asteroid to the planet."

The good news is we have many, many ways to fix this problem. The question is: do we have the collective will to do it fast enough?

MOVING FROM AWARENESS INTO ACTION

"What about you and me? We can use your money and my eye, and we can make films to expose the destruction going on in our oceans."

Louie's growing appreciation for the urgency of this crisis and his decision to launch OPS came from a convergence of events. At one point he shot a photo essay for Fortune Magazine featuring Jim Clark, a computer genius and entrepreneur who became a billionaire by founding several Silicon Valley technology firms. The two became friends and then diving buddies, eventually teaming up to do underwater photography at dive locations around the world. Over the years they began to notice that each time they returned to a diving location, they would see far fewer fish. One of those locations was the Galapagos Islands where they also observed fishermen poaching sharks in a marine sanctuary.

One day Jim Clark was visibly upset about the situation, and told Louie, "Someone should do something about this."

Louie agreed. He looked at Jim seriously, and asked, "What about you and me? We can use your money and my eye, and we can make films to expose the destruction going on in our oceans." In that moment, a partnership was born.

For Louie, it was a huge and risky departure, both personally and financially, moving from a life as a still photographer to a life as an activist producer of documentaries. Exposing illegal activities can be dangerous, especially when big money is involved, and it's often as dangerous to expose legal ones. Yet, in his view, the stakes of not doing so were far beyond reason. He felt he had a moral imperative to let the world know what was happening and a responsibility to motivate as many people as possible to change it.

Their partnership took form in 2005 when Jim Clark bankrolled the startup of the non-profit OPS and the making of its first film, *The Cove*. The film would expose the widespread slaughter of dolphins in Tajai, Japan, the sale of the most attractive dolphins to theme parks, and the serious health threat to the Japanese population who were ingesting incredibly high levels of mercury in dolphin meat.

Louie knew he would need to collaborate with a team to fulfill his mission. As he puts it, "I had a bunch of my buddies with me. We weren't filmmakers, either. I took a three-day course on how to make a film before I went to Tajai, Japan to shoot *The Cove*."

Fully aware of what he *didn't* know, he called upon close friends in the movie business like Paula DuPre' Pesmen, an Associate Producer on the first three Harry Potter movies. Paula knew the mechanics of how to make a film. He also brought on Fisher Stevens, an actor, director, writer, and movie producer.

Making that film was far riskier than Louie first anticipated, and he received death threats for doing so. From the moment he and his team arrived in Tajai to start shooting, they discovered they were being followed, but had no idea by whom. As he says in the film, "We didn't know if it was whalers, Japanese mafia…we had no idea." The chase continued throughout the entire filming in Japan, forcing Louie and his crew to shoot the footage at night and from hidden locations in daytime hours.

The film crew, with Louie Psihoyos directing, employed a host of undercover tactics and gadgets to secretly film everything from the bloody mass slaughter of thousands of dolphins in a secret cove to the donation of mercury laden dolphin meat to local school children.

The Cove was an overwhelming success, one that would earn a slew of awards around the world, including an Academy Award for Best Documentary for co-producers Louie Psihoyos and Fisher Stevens. Most importantly, the film achieved its purpose of educating the world about the needless destruction of marine life that was leading to its very demise.

THE CHALLENGE IS NOT TOO BIG TO SOLVE

"Scientists are more in the place where they are shouting that the house is on fire, and they are measuring the temperature of it."

Perhaps the greatest hurdle Louie Psihoyos faces is the sense that this issue can feel too big for people to absorb; it feels overwhelming so they often block it out or shut down emotionally.

"People think they can't do anything about it. Paleontologists feel as if they are trying to educate people, but no one is acting fast enough or with enough urgency. They are trying to raise awareness and educate people, but inspiring people to take action is the most difficult part.

"Scientists are more in the place where they are shouting that the house is on fire, and they are measuring the temperature of it. I want to throw buckets of water on the fire. So for me the question is, *how* do you inspire people to take action?"

The Cove was an excellent answer to that question. Because the film focused on the direct and visible destruction of ocean life, not the secondary or indirect effect of carbon dioxide, meaningful change occurred as a direct result of people watching that film. The demand for dolphin meat across Japan plummeted an astonishing 60% and is no longer served in school lunches. That impact is massive, and it matters, not only because the drop in the market for dolphins was precipitous, but also because mercury is the most toxic, non-radioactive element on earth, so potent it causes severe brain damage. And yet, prior to viewing *The Cove*, people in Japan had no knowledge of what they were ingesting.

As important as that accomplishment was, *The Cove* had a far wider impact. Other organizations piggybacked on the success of the film in the best possible way. The film *Blackfish*, which reveals the dangerous ramifications of capturing and holding captive killer whales for human entertainment, was written and produced by a friend of Louie's, Gabriela Cowperthwaite. Released four years after *The Cove*, *Blackfish* became an enormous success, and its impact in reducing support for capturing and holding mammals is still being realized. Louie couldn't be happier about the success of *Blackfish*, and the impact that both films created.

"I think we are saving about 10,000 cetaceans a year as a result of these films", Louie says, with a smile that reveals his deep satisfaction of making a material difference in the world. Cetaceans are one of the most communicative and intelligent mammals, and include the blue whale, dolphins, humpback whales, and about 80,000 other species.

The success of *The Cove* was a powerful affirmation that people do want to know what is going on, and they are willing to take steps to make change. They need to be informed of the truth, they need to feel the impact of that information, and they need to understand what they can do personally. Movies are a powerful medium that can easily educate viewers, reaching broad swaths of individuals, organizations, governments, and activists who can then take it to the next level.

"Nothing will motivate people like a film, where viewers have ninety minutes in a dark theatre away from their phones. You can really take them on a ride if you have a good story, and really change their hearts and minds. We had enough intellectual content in *The Cove* to make a case, but you need to make a case that makes people feel. If you don't get at their emotions you can't create change. You know, scientists hate that—but it's why they are so many are ineffective at impacting people."

Louie hopes his latest film, *Racing Extinction,* will be a true game changer for society. Five years in the making, the film exposes the ongoing, extensive ecological damage wrought by our addiction to oil and gas, and also exposes the underbelly of the international wildlife trade responsible for the outright killing of endangered species. The film makes known exactly where and with whom the responsibility lies.

Taking it a step further than *The Cove, Racing Extinction* reveals how all of us living in the modern world contribute to the degradation of our planet. Using a special camera fitted with a filter that makes carbon dioxide visible to the naked eye, viewers are suddenly confronted with its ubiquitous sources—they can see with their own eyes what's harming our planet. Being able to actually see the gas emitting from planes, cars, smokestacks—even innocuous looking leaf-blowers—helps viewers understand the many sources of deadly carbon emissions that are warming our climate to dangerous levels.

"The camera is a game changer. It allows the world to see what scientists have been talking about for decades. It's real, it's out there, it's in our everyday life."

Coupling their efforts with *The Discovery Channel,* the team extensively uses social media to encourage direct action from viewers. The collaboration is making the film a springboard for meaningful change. Several other critically important partners were also brought in to help spread the message.

"We start our film looking at the big, charismatic mega fauna, the dolphins that are about to go extinct, and the whales, which are vulnerable for a lot of different reasons. Then we go to a plankton conference, which almost sounds like a joke, you know, people getting together to discuss plankton—until you realize how crucial it is to all life on the planet. The ones who understand it, those who draw a line between where we have been, where we are, and where we are going, see this great collapse coming. So we are making sure people know and understand this, and most importantly, take action.

"In *Racing Extinction,* we focus on the oceans, because that's what we do. But everything is related. Depictions of the food chain today look like a spirograph, showing how connected everything in life is. So you might ask, what the hell do we need bees for? And then we discover they pollinate 40% of the things we eat. And we are having this collapse of the bee population because of pesticides and monocrops."

Louie explains that the collapse of many ecosystems is imminent, relatively speaking. "There are four primary drivers of extinction: overconsumption, habitat destruction, pollution, and invasive species. The oceans get hit by every one of them. And some regions get hit harder than others. So we focus on the oceans primarily. We do the undercover work to expose things that are going on that are wrong and that people simply aren't aware of. When you can take people underneath, then you don't have to explain. They say a good documentary tells, a great one shows. We try to show as much as possible. One thing we focus on in *Racing Extinction* is the illegal wildlife trade. We did some undercover work to expose people selling highly endangered species, and those people are making a lot of money profiting off these animals that are probably facing the last one or two generations."

Louie Psihoyos photographing shark fins drying on a rooftop in Hong Kong.
Killing sharks for their fins, which are used to make shark fin soup,
is the primary reason the species is going extinct.

CREATING A BIGGER AUDIENCE

"I know it all sounds overwhelming. But if we all just start with one thing, we can start a movement."

In addition to the *Discovery Channel's* robust decision to show *Racing Extinction* in multiple time slots in more than 220 countries and territories around the world, as well as to make it available for purchase from many vendors across a host of formats, Louie Psihoyos knows there are many people who still won't have the opportunity to see it.

This is exactly why OPS and partnering organizations came up with a really, really big idea to get the word out about extinction and climate change. Wanting to reach the greatest possible number of viewers, OPS teamed with other big thinkers at Obscura Digital, Vulcan Productions, and others to create *Projecting Change*, a multimedia experience that projects images of endangered species on some of the largest, most iconic structures in the world.

Combining haunting music, stunning National Geographic photos of endangered animals, and a display of the causes of mass extinction, they project the message: *The whole world is singing…but we've stopped listening.* The dramatic images also included melting icecaps and dying coral reefs to drive home the message, which is also verbally delivered by Jane Goodall. Her message includes a call for education and the restoration of hope, adding that "If we all lose hope there is no hope, and without hope people fall into apathy. There is still a lot left worth fighting for."

Among other messages the projection includes: *Now is the time. It's time to lead. Mobilize political will. Solutions exist. Put a price on carbon. Tomorrow is too late for the planet.*

'Illuminating Change' projected on the Empire State Building

Kicking off the effort with a projection on the United Nation's General Assembly building in New York, OPS and their multiple partners in the project followed up with a forty-story tall projection on the Empire State Building, grabbing the attention of millions more viewers. Not content to stop there, Louie teamed with Elon Musk of Tesla Motors to design a portable projection option that will allow them to take the message on the road. The result was a customized, all-electric Tesla Model S vehicle equipped to project the images on large and small surfaces all across America.

Their latest projection, however, brought the message to a new audience in an old world, when Louie's team received the blessing from Pope Francis to project the light show on St. Peter's Basilica in Rome.

'Illuminating Change' projected on St. Peter's Basilica in Rome.

These locations are so well known and visible that millions of viewers have seen *Illuminating Change*. The message from Louie Psihoyos, his OPS team, and collaborating partners is crystal clear: *You now know this is real. You cannot pretend it is not happening, or that you don't know that it is happening. It is up to each of us and to all of us to change our lifestyles and influence our leaders to create change immediately.*

After seeing the film, each viewer is challenged to take personal action, which is also promoted on social media with the hashtag, **#Startwith1Thing**.

Using a website by the same name as the film, *Racing Extinction.com*, options where viewers can each make a difference are presented in many areas, from changing our diet and our energy use, to making informed seafood choices, to altering or reducing our transportation usage. There are interactive quizzes to measure one's own impact on the environment, opportunities to learn more about and help specific animals, sign petitions, and more. The website also presents options for taking it up a notch, suggesting ways to challenge the city where you live to go green, and even helps viewers select a hybrid car. It's a powerful way to ask viewers to be more than viewers—to take action to change the outcome of what they have just witnessed and learned.

"I know it all sounds overwhelming. But if we all start with just one thing, we can start a movement."

PERSONAL RISKS, PERSONAL RESPONSIBILITY

"If you are doubling your output with a substance that is half as polluting, you are still in the same place. You won't be reducing it when the demand doubles."

It's quite rare for the Executive Director of a non-profit to face serious personal risks. However, while the nature of OPS is to inform and inspire the public, the work inherently takes aim at those most responsible for creating damage to the oceans.

"When we did *The Cove* we had death threats. Some were made by people who had never even seen the film and assumed it was a Japan-bashing movie when, in truth, I think it's more of a love letter to Japan. The dolphins that were being force-fed to schoolchildren were off-the-charts toxic with mercury. That's why I say it's more of a love letter to the culture since it ended up stopping that practice—not bashing the culture.

"In the *Racing Extinction* film, we are taking on the fossil fuel industry, and they can be pretty nasty. We are confronting them at the very foundation of their business. I would love to bankrupt them all if they don't switch over to renewable energy sources. The problem is they have the infrastructure in place to make a lot of money at the expense of the environment."

Louie doesn't mince words when discussing the issue directly with oil and gas executives either. Once, when attending a luncheon in Aspen, he was seated next to the president of a major U.S. oil company. The man was touting his company's recent shift to producing more natural gas and less oil, which he argued was a help to the environment. Louie told him point blank, "We have scientists who are looking out fifty years and 5 million years, and if you burn all the oil and gas that you are talking about, we aren't going to have any coral reefs in just forty years. How do you reconcile your short-term business interests with the long-term economic and environmental damage you're doing?"

The executive responded that natural gas is only half as polluting as oil. Louie responded, "If you are doubling your output with a substance that is half as polluting, you are still in the same place. You won't be reducing it when the demand doubles."

The oil company executive then asked Louie, "Well, where do you get your energy?"

Louie replied, 'I drive an electric car and I installed solar panels on my home for energy."

The man shrugged and responded, "Well not everyone can afford that."

This is a common belief, but it doesn't hold water as Louie sees it. "Solar panels are 75% cheaper than when I installed them six years ago. And they are extremely effective and cost saving."

In fact, he ends up selling the excess energy he captures with solar panels back to the local energy company. He actually *makes* money each month, rather than paying a gas or electric bill. And he does it without adding to global warming.

He also believes you can't quantify the benefits of these greener choices by money alone, citing other benefits of using alternative energy even in addition to protecting the environment.

"Once you have driven an electric car, you just can't imagine driving anything else. It's like once you have a smart phone, you can't imagine texting with an old phone that requires you to press a button three times to get one letter."

In addition to using solar power to heat our homes and electricity to power our vehicles, Louie has other suggestions for ways that individuals can act personally to save the oceans, and hence, the planet.

"I'd invite them to adopt a plant-based diet. It is seven times more polluting to have an animal-based diet. Not to even mention the suffering to animals, but just the cost to the environment. So if you want to save the oceans, become a vegetarian or a vegan."

Few people really want to hear that, however.

"When you start messing with what people eat and what they drive, and how they get their energy…well, we aren't in this to make friends. But it's not enough to talk about stuff. You have to do stuff. Awareness is critical, but it's only step one."

As the movie points out, it's not an all-or-nothing proposition. If every American skipped meat and cheese just one day a week for a year, it would be like taking 7,600,000 cars off the road. And installing solar panels on your home could save enough fuel to drive a car more than halfway around the world each year. Those changes are relatively easy, and yet the impact is tremendous.

"I have to be an example to myself. So I try to make my own life as green as possible, so I can walk the talk. That leads me to a point where my life choices and my mission have sometimes gotten in the way of my relationships. It's not that I only want to hang out with vegans, but I do want to have people around me who understand and live the mission, and don't just talk about it."

That realization led him to establish OPS as a vegan workplace, meaning only plant-based food is allowed on the premises. It's a strong message, and perhaps a risky one, but clearly he reached a point where he had to enforce his own guideline to stay in alignment with his core beliefs about preserving the environment.

PASSION AND COMPASSION

"There's a ripple effect that goes on around the world, and you inspire more and more people."

Louie believes that in order to lead and inspire change, and be successful at it, you have to be both passionate and compassionate. That applies to businesses and non-profits where leaders are working many long hours in what is often a thankless situation.

"I would add this—if you are doing business to make money for yourself, that's only going to go so far. That's pretty empty. When your circles of compassion get bigger, and expand outward, I think you can get more support. And the financing does seem to magically appear, because you are supporting the universe in a very positive way.

"The rewards are amazing. *The Cove* was one of the most decorated documentaries of all time. It swept all the film guilds. We won nearly 100 awards around the world; we won Sundance, and an academy award. And when you to start to see the impact—like the woman who bankrolled *Blackfish* who credited her inspiration from *The Cove*—eventually she also became a vegan. There's a ripple effect that goes on around the world, and you inspire more and more people."

So, while Louie holds passion and compassion as the two most important pieces in making an impact, what's the third?

"I hire people who are smarter than me."

FACING DIFFICULT REALITIES AND STAYING THE COURSE

"I don't get despondent over that, I get empowered. If we don't do it, well then who the hell is going to do it?"

One approach Louie cites for staying motivated is surrounding himself with people who are taking action. "If you look at *The Cove*, and the way it's constructed, you almost have a feel of an Oceans 11 team, where everyone is an activist with a specialized skill. In *Racing Extinction*, we highlight people who are doing incredible things. For example, we have Elon Musk, who started Tesla Motors, and we have a Tesla as a getaway car. Elon is the biggest installer of solar in the country. He's considered the real-life Iron Man, the real life Tony Stark. Working with people like him who take decisive action keeps me inspired."

While watching the bloody slaying of dolphins en masse in *The Cove* is painful and difficult, Louie believes that rather than bringing viewers down, it actually inspires them. It shows that a small group of committed people can make a huge difference. Referencing the well-known quote by Margaret Mead, he adds, "It's the only thing that ever has".

"Here's the exciting thing about where humanity is as a species. When my generation was growing up, we didn't know we were screwing it up. Maybe a few rare individuals like Rachel Carson knew, but the culture wasn't up to speed on the scale of the damage being done. By the time my kids have kids, it will be too late. They can't do anything. The generation that's alive right now is the only generation that can really fix it. We are deciding the fate of the planet. This generation is determining the fate of not only humanity, but the fate of millions of species for eternity. I don't get despondent over that, I get empowered."

SHARON CONTENT
Founder, Children of Promise, NYC

EMPOWERING CHILDREN OF INCARCERATED PARENTS TO BREAK THE CYCLE

"If you are separated from your parent by divorce, by military deployment, or even death, society has a level of sympathy and compassion. 'Oh, your mother is in Afghanistan;' 'Oh, your mother passed away.' There's a level of sympathy for those children. If you have a parent in prison, that level of sympathy doesn't exist. These young people bear the burden of their parent's crimes."

Despite our age of full disclosure and twenty-four-hour news cycles, some secrets still endure. Nearly three million children in the United States have a parent in prison and the majority of those kids are keeping it a secret—from their friends, from their schools, even from their relatives. With no empathy, no services, and no support, it's a mental health nightmare for these children left behind, seventy percent of whom are likely to end up in prison themselves.

Not only do the children keep their secrets—society does as well.

This massive population of children whose parents are incarcerated has long been hidden or ignored, creating a powder keg that continued unabated until Sharon Content stumbled upon it, blowing the lid off the secrecy and charting a path to change it. She is devoting her life to creating an emotionally and physically safe place for these silent sufferers to thrive and heal, an effort also intended to help them grow into productive citizens who reject—rather than replicate—the mistakes their parents made.

By founding *Children of Promise*, an after-school program and summer camp in New York City open to youth with one or two parents in prison, Sharon Content has virtually rewritten their present and their future. She is working to take the concept nationwide and provide much needed support to all children of incarcerated parents. It's a mission that couldn't be more satisfying, or further removed, from her original career path on Wall Street.

WHEN WALL STREET LOST ITS LUSTER

"When I first started working on Wall Street, the money was great, the guys looked good in their suits, and it was a hot, sexy place to work after college."

Sharon Content stood in the ladies restroom at the Smith Barney Investment offices on Wall Street. Something was wrong. As she scrutinized her reflection in the mirror, her face appeared tight, her expression, somber. Walking back toward her office, she couldn't help but notice her co-workers levity as they chatted. They reminded her of how she had felt just five years earlier, when everything at work was new and exciting, when she loved every facet of her job.

Now, she felt uninspired and out of sync with the world of finance she engaged in every day. Wall Street hadn't changed. Something inside Sharon, had.

"When I first started working on Wall Street, the money was great, the guys looked good in their suits, and it was a hot, sexy place to work after college. I loved being there. I got into the Brooks Brothers suits—believe me. Then one day I suddenly realized, *this is just not satisfying at all.*"

With no end game in mind, she quit her job at Smith Barney with only one clear goal: she wanted to make a positive impact on the world.

"My parents are still alive and still together, retired and living in Coral Springs, Florida. I grew up in the suburbs of Queens. I went to college, and my road map was kind of set for me. I was truly blessed and fortunate because I was born into that circumstance. I wanted to help level the playing field for kids who were not nearly so fortunate. I wanted to use my time, energy, and skills to work in a low-income, urban community. I just didn't know where to begin."

Sharon began her search for a more meaningful life by following her intuition and trusting the answers would come. After leaving Wall Street, she immediately volunteered for United Way, a nationwide coalition of charitable organizations, which gave her exposure to a wide variety of community-oriented endeavors.

She found her first paid job teaching entrepreneurship to troubled youth at an alternative-to-incarceration program, meaning the young people had committed a crime, and had to either attend the program or go to prison. Though she was a mother of two young children by then, she had no experience working with teens. They hired Sharon based on her business experience and accounting skills, and tasked her with creating micro-businesses where young people could find work.

Almost immediately, a new level of satisfaction engulfed her and Sharon knew she had found her calling—introducing troubled youth to a life filled with options they didn't know existed.

"When I left that first job I told them, 'Thank you for helping me find my calling in life!' I was 27, and I had discovered my real purpose!'"

In her next job, a traditional after-school program for boys and girls in the South Bronx, Sharon quickly rose to the position of Chief Operating Officer, managing thirteen sites serving 3000 young people a day. It was there she discovered the dearth of resources for children left behind when mothers and fathers were arrested and sent to prison.

"Even if someone is tough on crime and believes the adult should pay their debt to society, no one thought of that person as a mom who had three kids? No one asked, 'What's going to happen to her children?'"

In the eight years that passed as she worked for these two organizations, Sharon came up against this same problem again and again, with no options and no resources to offer the children left behind.

"Let's say you get arrested at 2 o'clock in the afternoon and you are taken to the police station. No one asks, 'Do you have children? Whose going to pick them up from school?' Or, when they are being sentenced, the judge usually does not consider what will happen to the person's children during their incarceration. That's just not relevant in the criminal justice system along the lines of sentencing, or along the lines of, 'How do we help the family who is being left behind?' There is no person, no group, no agency responsible."

SHAME, SECRECY, AND THE LOSS OF A PARENT

"The parent-child relationship is the most important relationship of any being, of any species. So you can imagine a child losing their parent and not being able to be open about it with other individuals."

The impact of a parent's incarceration is a traumatic event and always devastating for the prisoner's child in multiple ways. Besides losing the one, and sometimes two, people in the world who love and care for them, children left behind face a society that rejects them. Not only are they often thrust into foster care with a complete stranger, they also face a unique combination of trauma, shame, and stigma. Their parent's prison sentence becomes their own form of incarceration, albeit outside metal bars.

The stigma of shame can fester when other family members ask the children to hide the fact that their mother or father is in prison, creating additional mental health problems.

"The grandma or aunt who is raising them may say, 'Now don't say anything when you go to school. Don't mention it to anyone that Mom got arrested, or Mom is in prison.' So, as a result, teachers often don't know, guidance counselors don't know, and the child lives with the secret.

"The parent-child relationship is the most important relationship of any being, of any species. So you can imagine a child losing their parent and not being able to be open about it with other individuals."

The numbers of children suffering with the shame and the pain of abandonment are staggering. In New York State prisons, nearly 75% of incarcerated women are mothers of children under the age of 18, and 60% of incarcerated men are fathers of children under 18 years, meaning the vast majority of the people in prison are parents. Considering the country as a whole, the situation is truly troubling. 2.7 million children have at least one parent in prison, a number that has skyrocketed in the past 25 years. International human rights advocates believe that parental incarceration is the greatest threat to the wellbeing of children in the United States.

The stigma and societal rejection these children face often manifests in negative or even tragic ways. In a recent segment of America Tonight that featured Children of Promise, children of incarcerated parents were asked how they were dealing with their situation. One young boy recalled "blacking out with rage" at school and fighting other students, not able to process the emotional distress and abandonment he felt. Michael, an 8-year old whose mother was serving time for committing a violent crime, said, "I brought a weapon to school because I thought if I did what my mom did, that then I'd be able to be with her."

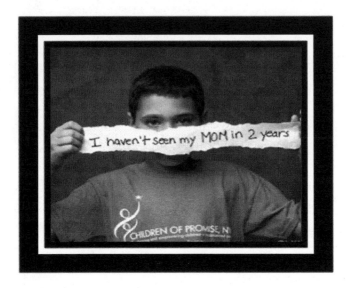

"If you are separated from your parent by divorce, by military deployment, or even death, society has a level of sympathy and compassion. 'Oh, your mother is in Afghanistan;' 'Oh, your mother passed away.' There's a level of sympathy for those children. If you have a parent in prison, that level of empathy doesn't exist. These young people bear the burden of their parent's crimes."

As Sharon Content pondered the situation, her frustration grew. She discovered more than 105,000 children in New York state alone had parents in prison, some with sentences over 25 years. It was clear things had been this way for a long time, and if she wanted to change the experience for those children she would need to do it herself. She understood the problem; she also had an idea of what the solution might look like. Still, she would trudge along for a long time until her plan clarified and began to take form.

Ultimately, Sharon decided an after-school program, coupled with a full-time summer camp, would be the best way to provide support, opportunity, and safety for the children left behind. Above all, Sharon wanted to provide the children with two main supports: camaraderie with other children suffering the same negative emotions and stigmas, and, mental health counseling to deal with the unique and often-severe psychological trauma they were experiencing.

It would take two years for her idea to take form. In 2009, *Children of Promise NYC* opened its doors to 200 boys and girls with one or two parents in prison. Every day after school they could attend a program that offered them a whole new world of camaraderie and companionship where they could be honest about their lives and open about their needs.

Though they couldn't have known it then, their lives were about to change in very dramatic ways. A physical and emotional safety net had suddenly appeared for all these children who had had no support, nor understanding, nor help since the day their mother or father was sent to prison. And, because every child entering the program was in the same situation, their comfort level with one another was immediate. It would take time, however, to overcome their deep sense of shame.

LISTENING AND LEARNING

"They can talk about what it means to not have their mom or dad there, or what its like to drive eight hours and visit their parent behind glass; to visit

him or her and then drive back and deal with the depression, and the loss, and the anger of not having their parent in their life."

Once programming began, Sharon listened as the young people and their caregivers shared their challenges with her. Those sessions began to strongly guide the development of the program and its continuous evolution.

"I originally thought we would use an outside social worker to deal with their personal issues. But after three years, I realized, it's just not going to cut it. In the African American and Latino communities, mental health services are not seen as part of the healing process. I would make an appointment for a child to see a mental health worker and they wouldn't go. So what could I do with that?"

Sharon decided the best answer would be for Children of Promise to become a licensed mental health center. "I thought, 'Let them get counseling from someone they already trust.'

"We began the process with interns—students who were earning a Masters of Social Work from some of the best schools in New York, including Fordham University, Columbia University, and Hunter, one of the campuses of City University of New York. We got great MSW interns! We had a clinical social worker and a part-time psychiatrist to supervise. With that process we were able to provide mental health counseling before we were licensed. It wasn't difficult to figure out how to do it, but getting funding for it? That was the challenge! There was no Medicaid reimbursement – nothing! My goal was to provide the services I felt were really going to create a change in the young people. We had to do it at that level."

Though it took years of work to accomplish, today *Children of Promise* is a licensed mental health clinic offering professional counseling not only to the children in the program, but to their caregivers and other family members as well. Sharon sees the process as a holistic model, and every part of the child's life must be considered and supported in the same way.

To keep support alive year round, Sharon added a summer day camp to avoid a long summer lag with the potential to reverse all they had learned.

"We have a very innovative model and we are very unique. We look like a traditional after school program and summer day camp to a person just coming in. That is by design. We want it to look like and be a fun, safe after school and summer camp program. The difference is that we infuse mental health into all aspects of the program. So, in addition to recreation and academic support, dance, theatre, basketball, soccer, and computer labs—in addition to all that—we also have group counseling, one to one counseling, music therapy, therapeutic art, and spoken word [poetry]. These are all activities that allow the young people to deal with the challenges of having a parent in prison. They are activities designed to deal with the emotional, physical, and social aspects of having a parent who committed a crime, to deal with the stigma and mental shame around that.

"The youth don't see these activities as therapy. They don't see it as going to a *special place*. They see it as their after-school program. 'Some kids go to Boys and Girls club, some kids go to YMCA, I go to Children of Promise.'"

For group sessions, students are placed in very small age groups so that six and seven year olds meet together, eight and nine year olds meet, and so on. They can talk about what its means to not have your mom or dad there, or what it's like to drive eight hours and visit your parent behind glass; to visit him or her and then drive back and deal with the depression, the loss, and the anger of not having their parent in their life.

"If the child is even able to express, 'My mom is in prison serving ten years,' it would be something. They don't even say it! They don't even have the opportunity to divulge the situation without a level of shame and the stigma associated with it.

"Our kids are dealing with challenges. So the organization is designed specifically to deal with these challenges so they can break the cycle. That's our goal—to break the cycle of incarceration; to not have these kids end up in the criminal justice system. And how do we do it? We could offer the best SAT prep, have the most chaperoned trips and academic support or the best sports program, but unless we tackle the problems from the inside out, we are not really providing the service that I want to provide. Our counseling has made all the difference in the world."

In July and August, the same two hundred children attend full day summer camp where they play chess, enjoy arts and crafts, participate in therapeutic art, dance, and drama, always with group counseling in the mix. Other days they learn to swim, skate board, or even surf.

Sharon Content has learned to use collaboration with other local groups as a way to expand the options for the youth. A partnership with New York Bikes allows groups to go to the West Side highway and ride bikes for two hours. Girls Scouts of America brings in Brownies and Daisies. New York Cares provides a literacy program. The list is extensive.

THE FUNDING CHASE

"I was stunned! I was speechless! Then I started crying."

Like nearly all non-profits, securing sufficient funding for Children of Promise is an ongoing challenge. Competition is stiff for state and federal government funds, which provide 90% of current support. *Children of Promise* competes for funding with giant organizations such as Boys and Girls Clubs. Only 5% of the budget comes from individuals, a situation Sharon Content is working to increase.

A story helps illustrate one of the many unique ways Sharon Content has raised funds. One day two men from California came to visit the center. They were filming a documentary, and told Sharon they would potentially like to include *Children of Promise* in their film. They planned to post the documentary on YouTube, but also said they would submit it to the Sundance Film Festival. Hesitant at first, but in need of funds, Sharon agreed to participate, thinking at least she would receive a video she might eventually be able to use in her fundraising efforts.

To begin, the two men wanted a film crew to follow a new volunteer around the organization. The filmmakers told her they would provide a volunteer. A bit shocked, and leery as well, Sharon insisted they use an existing *Children of Promise* volunteer. But the men insisted on bringing in their own. It became a point of some contention, as Sharon insisted her own volunteers would have greater rapport with the kids. After extensive discussions, they finally convinced her the film would be more convincing if they brought in their own volunteer, as it would be more realistic to follow a stranger coming in and discovering the operation from the ground up.

"So this guy shows up, and I introduce him to everyone. The next day, he shows up again, and again. Finally, after several days of volunteering, he reveals to me that he is actually a successful businessman—a millionaire, in fact. He told me he was deeply inspired by our program, by the difference it makes in the lives of these forgotten children. Then he hands me a check for $60,000, just like that. It turned out they were filming the whole thing for the TV show, *The Secret Millionaire*.

"I was stunned! I was speechless! Then I started crying. They were filming all this time, which I had completely forgotten about in that moment of receiving a much-needed donation of $60,000. It's hard to fool me with anything at the agency because I am so deeply bonded to every aspect of it, even more than I should be, you know?"

THE GREATEST GIFT OF ALL: CONNECTING KIDS WITH THEIR PARENTS IN PRISON

When incarcerated parents engage in the daily lives of their children, they have a reason and a reminder of what they are living for.

No matter how much help and support Sharon and her staff provide to the youth at her center, she knew the one thing that could strengthen them most would be connecting with their parent, despite the distance and hurt that looms large between them.

Sharon used the donation from *The Secret Millionaire* to purchase the one thing they needed most—a van to drive students to the prisons to visit their parents. With several prisons to visit, most of them located several hours away, it was cost and time prohibitive to rent a bus or make other provisions for the children to travel to visit their parents.

The van changed all of that. Today the *Children of Promise* website contains a sign-up sheet for families to visit their loved ones at any of 24 prisons in New York state, ranging from Sing Sing to Fishkill to Attica.

Incarcerated father and his daughter reunite,
from the CNN special, 'This is Life'.

To help foster relationships between children and parents and make them as strong as possible, Sharon and her staff use every available tool, including helping children write letters, setting up videoconferences, and providing parents with newsletters that keep them apprised of activities their children are engaged in.

This communication gives hope and comfort to parents and their child or children, sometimes rebuilding strained relationships, and other times just keeping them connected. When incarcerated parents actively engage in their children's lives, they have a reason and a reminder of what they are living for. One formerly imprisoned parent wrote about what the communication meant to him while he was still behind bars:

> "...Once the boys were stable in the program, I began to receive letters from them sent by CPNYC. I felt very happy that I was now getting mail on a daily basis from my boys, and I must say that the feeling was breathtaking. Along with the letters, I received Newsletters informing me on activities that were taking place within the program. The best Newsletter I received was when my son Pedro was featured with his mentor Josh, which was great. I showed everyone. On March 2, 2012, I was released from prison after serving 16 years, and my first stop was Children of Promise, NYC. It was the greatest experience ever getting to know Ms. Content along with all the other staff that joined me that day. As my boys continue to be a part of CPNYC, I must say that I will continue to advocate for such a great program."

Youth remain involved at the center even after their parent is released from prison. Mental health counseling is often needed even more as the parent tries to integrate back into the lives of the family from whom they were separated, often for many years.

In the center of the Children of Promise front hallway stands a wall labeled *Voices from Afar*. The wall highlights and honors the bond between parents and their children. Heartfelt letters from imprisoned parents are framed and displayed there, providing tangible reminders that the mistakes they made in their lives didn't change the love they feel for the children they left behind.

A note written from a father to his daughter reveals the deep regret and anguish many imprisoned parents experience. Because many are serving sentences over twenty years, it speaks of the greatest pain of all—entirely missing their son's or daughter's childhood.

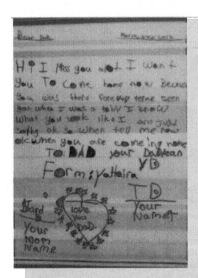

To My Daughter,

It has been years since the night my poor judgment removed me from your life. In an instant, my lack of discipline and commonsense, cost you the life every little girl is entitled to, to have a loving, caring father by their side to guide and protect them as they go through life. My actions caused you to have to pay the price for my wrong doings. That's not fair, and I am so very sorry.

I am sorry I wasn't there to teach you the things I should have taught you. How to ride a bike, shoot a basket or fly a kite. I wasn't there to help you learn to read and write, take you trick-or-treating, cook with you, play with you, or to comfort you when you were sad. I missed your first day of school, your first dance and too many birthdays and Christmases to ever make-up for. I've missed all the things that make you who you are, and I am so very sorry for that.

I would give anything to go back and be the father I should have been for you. I would pay any price to ease the pain I've caused you the slightest bit. I would do anything for one more chance to be the father I wish I was and that you deserve to have.

One thing that I hope you know and will always remember is none of this is your fault. You are the best part of my life, even though I'm not a part of yours now. You are a wonderful little girl and you will grow into a wonderful woman. You will have a wonderful life and hopefully have wonderful children of your own.

You are my every thought, my reason for the change I'm finally beginning to make. Please know that I love you with every ounce of my heart. You are my world.

Love,

TANGIBLE OUTCOMES KEEP HER INSPIRED

"One thing happens consistently in all of my visits to the prisons: the incarcerated parents thank me and Children of Promise for respecting their [parent–child] relationship."

While Sharon Content loves her job, and incarcerated parents love Children of Promise, the true measure of success is the impact on the children. The program began in 2009, so there are no long-term metrics of the impact on the youth. Nevertheless, there are tangible ways to measure short-term success.

One of the greatest indicators is this: 98% of all youth who attend the program return the following year. That figure alone speaks volumes. So does the fact that nearly all students choose to attend summer day camp as well.

Anecdotes of changed behavior are plentiful. Elijah was only 5 years old when his father was suddenly arrested and taken to prison. Elijah was angry and hurt, and unable to communicate about what had happened. Instead, he physically lashed out—at home, with friends, and at school. He was suspended from school nearly a dozen times.

"Then Elijah joined Children of Promise, NYC and learned how to use his words and not his fists. After years of confusion, he found his voice and joy again through counseling, art and music therapy, sports, and weekly letters to his father. Now, five years later, Elijah has a mentor, positive relationships with peers, and the motivation to resolve the challenging feelings surrounding his father's imprisonment."

The children's voices speak louder still. This is what one young boy shared about his experience:

"I've been here since the first day Children of Promise started. The first! I know that everyone in the program has the same situation as me. They have someone they knew, they loved and they cared for become incarcerated. Children of Promise taught me that I have other people who care for me, not just my father. Like everyone here—they care for me!"

An older teen says: "Children of Promise is somewhat of a savior. We can't even fathom what kind of life we would have without this place."

It's clear that everyone in the family of an incarcerated person, as well as the children's caregivers, benefit from the services offered by Sharon and her staff at *Children of Promise*. The greatest benefits of all may be the ones that Sharon never anticipated: strengthening and preserving the parent-child bond and sustaining the family in the face of overwhelming odds.

Sharon occasionally visits the prisons to meet parents of the children enrolled at Children of Promise. That's when she really gets to see the full picture of the program's impact, even beyond the benefits to the youth.

"One thing happens consistently in all of my visits to the prisons: the incarcerated parents thank me and Children of Promise NYC for respecting their [parent–child] relationship. While they committed a crime and are paying the consequences, they still love their children. They thank us continually for keeping their relationship with their child or children intact and ongoing while they are in prison."

USING SKILLS AND MONEY YOU HAVE—FIGURING THE REST OUT AS YOU GO

"I'm not selling a widget. People often think of a non-profit as a sub-level business, but I think it's much more challenging than a for-profit business."

Sharon's income plummeted when she decided to leave Smith Barney and work for a non-profit. When she started Children of Promise, her lower income turned into no income.

"For the two years it took me to develop the organization there was no income coming in. Luckily, I had a supportive husband, but it was still a two-income household where two incomes were needed, and one was missing for two years. So not only was there a reduction in salary when I finally got one, there were two years when I didn't make any money at all."

In addition to a plunge in income, the transition from the for-profit to the non-profit world presented challenges the public does not always understand nor appreciate. Having been accustomed to a workplace where the bottom line mattered most, Sharon was now working in a world where the impact she could make took center stage. Any money she raised was spent on increasing that impact. It's a different focus entirely.

"I'm not selling a widget. People often think of a non-profit as a sub-level business, but I think it's much more challenging than a for-profit business. Not only do you still have to do all the same things a for-profit does, all the marketing, the financials—everything a for-profit business does, but then you are also providing a free service, so you need to raise all the money for that. It's very, very challenging."

Sharon had a high level of confidence in her own abilities, which allowed her to believe that even though she couldn't see the path ahead, she would always be able to figure it out. She also knew that many of those answers would come from the process, from the people she was serving. For example, providing mental health services was not in her original plan. Adding it was a major undertaking, and she responded to the situation when it arose.

"You can have some idea where you are headed; you bring your experience and your knowledge and your expertise to the table, and you design what you think is best. But I believe that as an executive director, unless you are a part of that target population, you have to be open and accepting of how the families and the clients express their needs. I'm not a social worker, but I wanted these young people to get better. It became clear it had to be through providing mental health services. It couldn't come only through academic support or basketball."

SAGE ADVICE FOR WORLD CHANGERS

"Of all the people who are going through difficulty in this world, there must be something you can do outside your bubble! If everyone would do something, we would be phenomenal as a society."

"If you want to change something in the world, focus on the goal or the end in mind, then simply respect the process. The process is how you get there. Just think what outcomes you are seeking, keep that as your focus, and go through each step as it comes. Think with the end in mind. What impact do you want to make? Start with the result you want."

She warns people not to get caught up in negative thinking or disappointments. Disappointments are part of the process of getting what you want.

"In your projects, if you can stay focused on the euphoria of the outcome, on the end result, and recognize that everything along the way is just part of the process, you'll do fine. After I complete a huge grant and then find out we didn't get it, I don't get upset. I don't say, 'Damn! I didn't get it.' I just keep on going and think, 'Well, maybe we'll get the next one.'

"One process currently underway is gathering statistics and numbers to show to funders so we will to be able to replicate this model in this and other cities."

The outcome of that process, which means expansion to other locations in New York as well as expansion to cities across America, is a big part of Sharon Content's dream, one that is currently unfolding as they work to open a location in Harlem in 2016. After that, a nationwide expansion could follow. The process will determine that outcome.

While Children of Promise has grown and expanded, Sharon has also evolved, inspired by the program's success that she made happen. "I am totally committed to this model and to serving as many kids as possible. I wasn't expecting it to grow this big at the beginning. Now I have grown to want to impact as many, many kids as possible so they do not end up in prison."

Since the day Sharon Content opened Children of Promise, thousands of lives have been changed for the better. Whether one considers the children who are cared for, listened to, educated, loved, mentored, and rescued from the abyss of their own possible future incarceration, or the unknown individuals whose lives will not be harmed by crimes they will not commit, or the incarcerated parents who take comfort in knowing their children are cared for even though they made mistakes which have caused their own children to suffer, untold lives have been touched and made whole.

Sharon recognizes that everyone has different skill levels and that everyone brings their own unique gifts and abilities to the table. Regardless of what gifts one has, she firmly believes everybody can make a difference in some aspect of life.

"I think that if every person just chose something to do at a scale they can manage—whether it's donating an hour of time a week, or a month, or whether its giving $5 or $1,000 to a cause or charity they care about, everybody can do something."

She also recognizes that it takes a certain kind of person to start and run a non-profit organization.

"I knew when I started this organization that I was making a commitment on a certain level, and with my personality and the way I do things, I knew I would make a difference. People who start and lead non-profit organizations don't just have the personality and drive or the passion or the perseverance because of the organization they started. It doesn't happen like that. Those are personality traits they would bring to any endeavor. Most founders or executive directors address issues and challenges in their life in a certain way. I knew I was going to dedicate myself. I believed I would succeed."

Sharon never lost hope in the power of the individual to make a difference. In fact, she has restored her own belief in the future.

"I have hope for these young people, whereas I didn't before. I am very proud to be able to give them a voice, to articulate what I know our kids might not be able to. I feel very blessed by that."

Her frustration arises when people don't use their power, either because they lack confidence that they can, or because they lack the will.

"I just don't understand how anyone can have dedication to nothing but themselves and their family! It's just about you and your family? You give 110% to you and your family? Are you serious? Of all the people who are going through difficulty in this world, there must be something you can do outside your bubble! If everyone would do something, we would be phenomenal as a society."

Sharon's decision to start Children of Promise not only impacted thousands of lives and made them infinitely better; it did the same for hers.

"I get an income, and I get to do something I totally love every day. Every day I love what I do! I think that is a blessing; it's a blessing and I'm fortunate. Yes, I chose to do it in this way, and I don't know why everyone wouldn't choose that. It is so satisfying to wake up in the morning. I drive from New Jersey to Brooklyn every day—I drive from another state to get to work! And I tell the team, and the kids, how lucky I am to love my work.

"I work most with the teens, and we often talk about potential careers and their future. I tell them 'Do something that you love and are passionate about.' Because there is no single thing, no drug that would make me higher than I am when I come into work every day. I absolutely *love* what I do!"

NATHAN RUNKLE
Founder, Mercy for Animals

ENDING CRUELTY TO FARMED ANIMALS

"We're really battling this on the front lines rather than just putting a Band-Aid on a gunshot wound and trying to rescue just a few animals. Systemic change is precisely our goal."

Walmart, McDonald's, Butterball, Amazon, Dijorno, Nestle, Tyson, Chick-fil-A, Costco, the dairy industry, the egg industry, the veal industry, cattle ranchers, and pig farmers across North America all shudder when they hear the words "Mercy for Animals" and "undercover investigation" used together. They know that no amount of money, legal action, or personal threats can dissuade this inspired team from publicly exposing and engaging those who blatantly disregard animal welfare.

At 31 years of age, Nathan Runkle, the dynamic founder and President of Mercy for Animals, is working to change the system and the culture of how we raise and eat animals. He is not interested in being politically correct, passive, or ineffective. He is only interested in one thing: reducing suffering for the largest number of animals in the shortest amount of time.

Nathan Runkle never followed a traditional path in life, and since childhood, has consistently forsaken the status quo in favor of following his instincts. Whether confronting a biology teacher with no regard for animal suffering in the classroom, or taking on food industry giants when they choose cost savings over animal welfare, his road-less-travelled approach has routinely required raw courage and herculean efforts.

Through Mercy for Animals, the non-profit he founded at just fifteen years of age, Nathan continuously achieves significant victories, stunning in their reach and impact. Kraft, Nestle, Walmart, McDonald's, Costco, Butterball, and scores of others in the multi-billion dollar food industry have dramatically changed their practices or suppliers in response to pressure from Mercy for Animals. In addition to businesses, governments who fail to legislate protective laws or enforce existing ones also must contend with pressure from Nathan's large and growing animal protection staff, which includes professionals from many backgrounds working in several countries around the globe.

Focusing on four primary areas including undercover investigation, legal advocacy, corporate outreach, and education, Mercy for Animals seeks to "Expose cruelty, prosecute abusers, and inspire consumers to make compassionate food choices".

Nathan's path to activism began when he was just eleven years old. He was watching news coverage of a fur protest when he heard the term *animal rights advocate.*

"It was the first time I learned that people were standing up against actions I had been feeling were wrong all of my life."

UNUSUAL CLARITY OF PURPOSE

"There were many times I witnessed my uncles skinning animals alive as they were squirming and struggling to get away."

In the small Ohio farm town where Nathan Runkle grew up, nearly everyone raised or hunted animals for food, or worked for someone who did. Abstaining from eating meat was equivalent to rejecting the culture that defined and sustained nearly everyone who lived in his hometown, including his own family.

"My uncles were hunters, trappers and fishermen. There were many times I witnessed my uncles skinning animals alive as they were squirming and struggling to get away. All of this was just a part of growing up in our rural environment. It always felt wrong to me. I knew that when an animal was screaming in pain it just wasn't acceptable. So it was a journey I had to make on my own, to overcome the obstacles of living in a culture where there were no vegetarians or vegans and few animal advocates."

A few months after he discovered that animal rights activists existed, Nathan attended an Earth Day event where he visited a booth for an animal rights organization.

"I grabbed every piece of written information I could, one of which was on factory farming. I read that brochure in the car on the way home, and I just felt sick to my stomach. It was my first exposure to veal crates, battery cages, and gestation crates for sows."

While his first act of conscience was to stop eating animals, Nathan had no idea how to become a vegetarian other than to pick the meat out of his food at school. At home, however, it was a different situation altogether. Nathan's parents supported his choice not to eat animals, which eased the transition toward a vegetarian lifestyle. His mother began cooking vegetarian meals, often for the whole family. Given that Nathan was not yet old enough to drive, she and his father took turns escorting him to animal rights protests, even driving him from their tiny town in Ohio to attend an animal rights conference in Washington, D.C. By the time he was fifteen, Nathan was confident enough and supported enough to understand his life purpose and eventual career.

"I think a lot of kids know their calling and direction in life at a younger age than we tend to give them credit for. I was fortunate enough to have parents who were unwavering in their support of my sister and I, fully allowing us to choose our life paths and directions at very young ages."

Nathan would discover he was not alone in his empathy toward animals. He learned that many other children were suffering in silence, in particular his classmates and peers who participated in 4H clubs. 4H is an organization that, in part, helps educate and support youth who raise farm animals for consumption.

"I watched my fellow students raise pigs or cows. Many bottle-fed their animals. They became their best friends, their constant companions. Then one day, when the fair came around, they would take these animals in and watch them be auctioned off by the pound, and then sold. That bond would be physically broken as most of these children literally had their animal taken out of their arms. Often they were crying and distressed."

Nathan describes how a parent or person with the 4H program would tell the child, "That's just the way it is. You've got to buckle down and go along with it." Because Nathan was known as a vegetarian and involved in animal rights issues, a number of other young people in his community confided in him about how distraught they were and how they were struggling to rationalize and justify their participation.

"I think most children have a natural affinity towards animals. So many of the photographs of me as a child show me standing out in the yard holding toads, or turtles—all kinds of animals. I was always very connected to them. I found them fascinating, and spent a lot of time as a child with our dogs and cats; they're really the ones who taught me that animals have unique personalities and are very much like humans."

THE PIVOTAL EVENT

"The piglet still didn't die, and at this point her skull was fractured and she was bleeding out of her mouth; she was just in horrible distress."

One event moved Nathan from simply avoiding eating animals to becoming a force against harming them.

"The teacher brought a bucket of day-old piglets to be used in a dissection project in the class. These were piglets he had killed that morning on his farm. They were the runts—piglets that weren't going to grow for one reason or another. So he brought the piglets to school, and one of them was still alive. Another student in the class, who worked part-time on the teacher's pig farm, took the piglet by her hind legs and slammed her head first into the ground to try to kill her.

"The piglet still didn't die, and at this point her skull was fractured and she was bleeding out of her mouth; she was just in horrible distress. A few of the students in the class were shocked and appalled, outraged by this act of cruelty. They picked up the bleeding piglet and rushed it to another teacher who was known as being sympathetic to animals. She immediately drove the piglet to a local veterinarian's office to have it euthanized, as the piglet was clearly in horrific pain.

"Afterward, she filed animal cruelty charges against the student and the teacher involved. It was a really big deal in our community; it was on the local news and blazoned across the local newspaper."

Although the event occurred in his older sister's class, Nathan knew the teacher who drove the piglet to the vet as they had connected before around their concern for animal welfare. Kindred spirits living in a community where no one else spoke of such things, they joined forces to create an organization to raise awareness, naming it Mercy for Animals. The teacher remained involved for just a few months, but Nathan took it and grew it into the influential, international organization it is today.

Tragically, one year after he formed Mercy for Animals, Nathan's life changed dramatically when his mother died from breast cancer. He was just sixteen, and her death was devastating for Nathan. His mother had home schooled him for the prior six years in order to give Nathan the opportunity to professionally compete in figure skating. Though it was a sport he'd devoted his life to, at her death he shifted his full commitment to protecting animals.

Nathan's father, wanting to take care of his own health so he could be there for his children, and having long been influenced by his son, decided to adopt a vegan diet less than a year after his wife passed away. The health benefits were immediate, and his cholesterol plummeted 100 points. Later, his sister adopted a vegan diet.

When Nathan graduated from high school, he elected to forego a traditional higher education. He chose an alternate path, and for him, the decision was certain.

"There's not a Master's of Animal Advocacy degree, so I knew that with this very specific field and arena of what I wanted do, I would be better off learning hands-on, on the ground, getting experience, going to conferences, meeting others who had been involved in this work for a long time. That's exactly what I did. It was a nontraditional path, for sure."

FROM BABY STEPS TO
A MULTINATIONAL POWERHOUSE

"We're really battling this on the front lines rather than just putting a Band-Aid on a gunshot wound and trying to rescue just a few animals. Systemic change is precisely our goal."

When Nathan formed Mercy for Animals, he would never have imagined he would someday have the clout to force giant corporations into raising their treatment standards for farmed animals. Nor did he entertain the idea that *he* would be the reason Canada's top grocery chains stopped selling crated veal, or that Butterball, the world's largest producer of turkey meat, would be convicted of animal cruelty and fined as a result of Mercy for Animals' undercover video coverage.

He describes the organic growth of Mercy for Animals as a "One foot in front of the next" type of growth.

"It's really been in the last 6 or 7 years that we've been looking at the long-term strategic approaches. I started the organization initially because I really care about animals, but what I've learned is that it's very much about running a business in many ways. It doesn't sound sexy or glamorous to say that, but that's what it really is. What I've come to understand over the years is that MFA is largely a PR agency for farmed animals. We're looking to change public opinion, we're looking to change laws and corporations, and we're really battling this on the front lines rather than just putting a Band-Aid on a gunshot wound and trying to rescue just a few animals. Systemic change is precisely our goal."

Nathan's role in the organization has continued to grow and evolve since starting it. In the first several years, Nathan, quite literally, did everything.

"I would promote so many meetings, and often I would be the only person to show up, or perhaps one other person would show up. There were many public protests where I would be standing outside in the rain with just a few other people. I mean, it was very trying and very challenging, and it could also be very lonely at times. I just had to believe wholeheartedly in my mission, and believe that with enough work, determination, passion, and blood, sweat, and tears, things would start to improve and start to change."

Nathan's father supported him both financially and emotionally as he began to focus all his energy on building up Mercy for Animals. MFA applied for and received a non-profit status (501c3) in 2002, about three years into the process.

"It was almost a revelation at that point. I realized, 'Hey, we are going to need some money to help these animals! That's the way the world runs. So it's been an education on all fronts—not just fundraising, but technology, media, volunteer management and staffing—all of that. Organizations really are nonprofit businesses, so I think you have to quickly get into that mindset; what you're selling is social change."

"I'll be honest; I did a pretty lousy job of fundraising in the beginning, and I just sort of learned from my mistakes, and learned from others as I went along. I think the tipping point was when we had a few large donors who were willing to take a risk to invest, so I hired our second employee in 2006. That allowed me to step back a bit from the treadmill of the day-to-day work, like planning the next event, or figuring how to send out information, and really start to step back and look at bigger goals and objectives, strategies and fundraising. Once that happened, things started to build.

"MFA was definitely fueled by passion and ambition for quite a while, just being unrelenting and pushing forward and pushing for change. You know, there was a point when I had to say, 'I'm going all in on this, and I'm investing myself and my future, and it's not something that I will sort of do, maybe will do—it's actually—this is where I'm going to put myself, and there might be a number of years where it's not so easy. I think to really get something off the ground you have to be fully, 100% invested in it."

EXPOSING AND STOPPING ANIMAL CRUELTY

"Less than 24 hours after Costco executives saw our video footage, they contacted us. Soon after, they implemented a company-wide policy, stating they would not sell veal from producers who observe this cruel practice."

Mercy for Animals is best known for their undercover investigations, which involves sending double-agents into factory farms, slaughterhouses, hatcheries, and livestock auctions to obtain jobs like cleaning out cages. These courageous investigators are outfitted with hidden cameras, and they document what takes place inside. Investigations can run anywhere from 2 weeks to 3 months. Every single time they've sent in undercover investigators, they've encountered heartbreaking abuse.

Sometimes investigators are documenting legalized abuse. Many methods in the animal agriculture industry, like de-beaking baby chicks, are objectively cruel, yet remain standard and allowable practices. However, often they document malicious, sadistic abuse that is clearly illegal and can lead to animal cruelty charges. The investigations are the backbone of MFA's education campaigns, as they help generate media exposure that broadcasts factory farm images into the homes of people across the country.

"We live in a society where these huge multi-national corporations have the power to dramatically impact change. These companies are very vulnerable to public attack, and they want to protect their brand. So if we're able to do an investigation on a McDonald's egg supplier, and it's shown nationally on the news that they are supporting abusive practices, that can help force the hand of that major corporation to start making policy changes that will reduce suffering for animals.

"For example, we were able to get Kraft, the largest food and beverage company in North America, to implement a policy that phases out tail docking dairy cattle. Tail docking is a practice that involves cutting the tails off animals without any painkillers. It's cruel and it causes acute and chronic pain, and it's a practice the American Veterinary Medical Association stands firmly against. The dairy industry itself agrees. So, through our communications with Kraft, and through our investigation, we were able to implement this new policy, which is positively affecting millions of animals."

Among the worst forms of institutionalized animal abuse is the use of crates to house veal calves and pigs. MFA worked with Costco to ban the sale of veal from calves, which are kept in restrictive veal crates and chained by their necks to prevent moving around. That working relationship emerged as a direct result of an MFA undercover investigation of Costco's veal suppliers. MFA revealed the results with a press conference and public campaign.

"Less than 24 hours after Costco executives saw our video footage, they contacted us. Soon after, they implemented a company-wide policy, stating they would not sell veal from producers who observe this cruel practice."

A veal farm in Quebec was another prime target of an MFA investigation. Once undercover investigators secured damning video that revealed the horrific conditions baby calves lived in, they managed to broadcast the video along with an in-depth story on a major Canadian news channel. Subsequently, major Canadian newspapers published the story as well, forcing Canada's top grocery chains to end the sale of veal from crated calves by 2018. Quebec's veal producer's federation later announced they would also phase out the use of veal crates. It was a tremendous victory with huge implications for the treatment of baby calves.

While many individuals have chosen to stop eating veal in the past twenty-five years due to the cruel practices associated with calves, few have given up eating pork. Nathan explains it may be because they are unaware of the cruelty of gestation crates.

"In recent years there's been a lot of movement against the use of gestation crates for breeding sows. Gestation crates are two feet wide metal stalls that confine pregnant, breeding pigs. These pigs are kept there during their entire 4-month pregnancies. Once they give birth, they go right back into the stalls and they pretty much live their entire lives like this."

As Nathan characterizes it, "It's just really hell on earth for these animals. Pigs are highly intelligent, perhaps more so than dogs, and they are very curious. When they are placed in restrictive crates, it's physically painful for them because they can never move or turn around. Equally egregious, these intelligent animals have no mental stimulation, and no socialization."

Animal advocates, including and often led by Mercy for Animals, have successfully built a growing movement against the use of gestation crates for pigs in recent years. Over 30 major corporations have adopted a policy saying that they're going to phase out the use of these crates, and they have agreed not to sell pork that comes from producers who use them. That list includes some of the world's largest restaurants and grocery stores such as McDonald's, Burger King, Wendy's, Safeway, Costco, and K-Mart.

TAKING ON THE BIG BOYS

"The following day, the owners of that farm were charged with criminal animal cruelty."

Major corporations often react swiftly to tamp down negative press and protect their positions, but when they refuse despite months of conversation and pressure, MFA launches a targeted campaign in an effort to influence the company.

Walmart, the world's largest retailer, was one such holdout. They remained stubborn in their position and would not take positive action on this issue of abandoning suppliers who used gestations crates for pregnant sows. Despite multiple direct discussions between Mercy for Animals and Walmart, virtually no progress was being made.

Nathan and his staff launched a full-scale campaign educating Americans up-close in their own cities and towns. It was a tactic MFA used with other corporations to force a change in policy, one that worked successfully with

Amazon (*foie gras*), McDonald's (egg suppliers), Burger King (dairy suppliers), and Butterball (baby turkeys).

The Walmart campaign was exceedingly powerful. With films narrated by actor Joaquin Phoenix and *Titanic* Director James Cromwell, Mercy For Animals graphically and poignantly linked Walmart's obstinacy to the explicit torture of pigs. From the confinement of sows in filthy gestation crates to workers slamming piglets into the ground, from workers ripping out the testicles and slicing off the tails of piglets without any use of pain-killers to ignoring sick and injured pigs with wounds and infections, the films were a damning indictment of some of Walmart's suppliers' systemic infliction of cruelty.

For twelve weeks, the *Walmart Cruelty Tour* crisscrossed the United States, as MFA employees and volunteers transported a giant replica of a pregnant sow stuck inside a metal crate with images of sores and cuts splayed across her body. In 67 cities they staged protests as close as possible to local Walmart stores. Occasionally they encountered others who were protesting Mercy for Animals, but the campaign continued to raise awareness, and major media was always happy to spread the message.

Highly intelligent pregnant sows confined to crates chew on bars
continuously due to anxiety and frustration from never being able to move.

It would take a full two years, but victory arrived in June of 2015, when Walmart acknowledged the growing public concern for the humane treatment of farm animals. They announced new farm-animal welfare guidelines, stating: "Walmart will not tolerate animal abuse, supports the globally recognized 'Five Freedoms' of animal welfare, and is committed to working with its supply chain partners to implement practices consistent with the Five Freedoms."

Walmart announced it would ask its deli, dairy, egg, and meat providers to stop the use of pig gestation crates and other housing systems that keep animals confined in small enclosures, and to report and take disciplinary action against animal abuse.

They went a step further, asking suppliers to provide transparency on the issues by providing annual reports not only to Walmart, but to the public as well. Once again, the impact of more compassionate farming choices will reach millions upon millions of farmed animals.

REPEAT OFFENDERS

"She is unable to freely spread her wings, perch or roost, breathe fresh air or see the sun. Every natural instinct is frustrated, as these birds have been reduced to mere egg-producing machines."

Regardless of whether or not a company has succumbed to and accommodated the demands of Mercy for Animals in the past, it doesn't exempt them from future exposés. The wisest have learned not to rest on their laurels, as MFA will continue the pressure until all practices of animal abuse are eliminated. McDonald's is a case in point.

A recent *McCruelty* exposé showed workers at a chicken supplier moving live chickens by stabbing them with nail-imbedded clubs and tossing them into buckets. As the Wall Street Journal reported on September 9, 2015, "McDonald's has faced pressure from animal rights advocates to make its supply chain more humane. Last month, it dropped a poultry supplier after watchdog group Mercy for Animals documented abuse at a Tennessee farm that supplied chickens that were processed into McNuggets." The following day, the owners of that farm were charged with criminal animal cruelty.

It wasn't the first time MFA exposed cruel practices at McDonald's. In 2012, a campaign titled *McDonald's Cruelty: The Rotten Truth about Egg McMuffins*, was used to pressure McDonald's to stop buying their eggs from a supplier proven through undercover investigation to consistently engage in cruel practices. The most egregious charges focused on the use of tiny wire battery cages used to house the chickens.

MFA issued a petition, which read in part: "Although all of these are examples of intolerable cruelty...perhaps the worst form of abuse these birds are forced to endure is a life of prolonged misery in a tiny wire battery cage. Battery cages are so small that each bird has less space than a single sheet of notebook paper to live out nearly her entire life. She is unable to freely spread her wings, perch or roost, breathe fresh air or see the sun. Every natural instinct is frustrated, as these birds have been reduced to mere egg-producing machines."

HOW MFA MAKES CHANGE HAPPEN

"There is a real disconnect between how people think farm animals should be treated and the reality of the factory farms and the horrific conditions animals are subjected to."

To affect change in the powerful, multi-billion dollar food industry, Nathan and other MFA employees must be bold, aggressive, smart, creative, and exceedingly well prepared. They are.

MFA's highly educated and savvy staff of over thirty employees—along with a large, impassioned arsenal of interns and volunteers—has already won an astounding number of substantial, game-changing victories. Deeply motivated, they use the law, the press, petitions, celebrities, traveling campaigns, and education to make change happen fast.

In addition to investigations and exposure, MFA engages in legal advocacy efforts to force change. The focus is enforcing anti-cruelty codes and advocating for new laws that protect farmed animals on both state and federal levels. Currently no federal laws exist in the United States to provide protection to animals during their lives on factory farms. While there is a federal transport law, and a federal slaughter law, those laws apply primarily to pigs and cows yet exempt poultry, which makes up 95% of food production.

Nathan describes why this is such a problem. "Transport laws cover only the last few hours of those animals' lives. Because there are no federal laws, there's really no government oversight inside these factory farms, which is why this abuse is allowed to run rampant and go undetected, unchecked, and un-prosecuted. There are no USDA inspectors going into factory farms and observing the conditions of the animals because there is no law that they should even be looking."

While it may be the least flashy portion of their advocacy work, MFA also files complaints with the Federal Trade Commission about labeling and false advertising practices.

"It is critically important, because there is a tremendous amount of confusing and false labeling, creating a facade that animals are treated in a way that is more humane than the reality."

Like others who advocate making a difference, Nathan Runkle agrees education is the key to real and systemic change. MFA's educational component includes visiting schools to speak about animal agricultural issues and vegetarianism. It also includes targeted TV ad campaigns and educational materials to increase awareness and educate people about their food choices as they impact farmed animals.

"We think the baseline for all meaningful change on this issue comes from an informed constituent base, which demands change. Unfortunately, today most people are totally in the dark on how farmed animals are treated. They see ads on television about happy cows producing cheese, and happy chickens, and unfortunately that's just not the reality of how animals are treated. There is a real disconnect between how people think farm animals should be treated, and the reality of the factory farms and the horrific conditions animals are subjected to. So we put tremendous resources into consumer education."

A CHANGING TIDE

"When we have a victory, in many cases it can affect tens of thousands or even millions of animals."

MFA has been successful in contributing to cultural change as well as industry change. For example, in the past ten years, Americans have reduced meat consumption by ten percent, on average. Vegans and vegetarians now comprise 7% of the population, resulting in a doubling of retail demand and supply for vegetarian foods. That rate began to increase slowly a decade ago but now the growth is increasing exponentially, with the plant-based food sector becoming the fastest-growing segment of the food industry. Hampton Creek Foods, a Silicon Valley "food tech" company with an entirely plant-based product line, is currently the fastest growing food company in the world, drawing investments from Microsoft founder Bill Gates, venture capital giant Khosla Ventures, and the wealthiest man in Asia, Li Ka-shing. As a direct result of the dropping demand for meat, nearly 500 million fewer animals experienced the trials of factory farming and the horror of slaughterhouses in 2015.

Laws are also slowly changing to protect farmed animals, with the number of states enacting laws to ban veal crates, gestation crates, and battery cages increasing from one state to ten over the past decade. From a market perspective, many grocery stores, supermarket chains, restaurants and food-service companies have all pledged to remove crates or cages from their supply chains.

Though progress has been made, the road ahead remains long and steep. Still, every law passed to protect animals from abuse has a major impact.

"When we have a victory, in many cases it can affect tens of thousands or even millions of animals. You know that is not a small feat. You know when you get a piece of legislation passed, or force a corporate policy change, or even impact one person so they change their diet, it impacts such a large number of animals.

"That is so deeply rewarding."

TAKING IT PERSONALLY

"When we have an investigation, and we get video back of horrific animal abuse, it's disturbing for me to see, but I quickly turn that anger into activism and action steps."

Since Nathan literally grew up with the organization, he has had to find a way to occasionally separate himself from MFA, realizing he is his own person with his own interests outside the organization. The main reason for this compartment is preventing malaise and thus becoming less effective.

"There is a lot of burnout involved in the animal protection community, and I'm sure that that's true with all social issues, because they are difficult to work on. It's emotionally draining, and it's physically draining. Day after day you see heartbreaking images of animals being abused; you're being faced with the darkest side of humanity, seeing the very worst of what we're capable of doing. At the same time, you are trying to push for positive change and being met with a lot of resistance. That can take a toll on a person. I see activists get involved in the animal movement who are on fire with passion for the first year or two, and then have that passion extinguished because their souls have almost been broken when they realize how big of an issue it is."

Nathan takes a long-term view on animal protection issues, recognizing it is a battle that's going to continue on for a long time.

"It's good to mark our progress and our successes, and know that there are long-term goals and there are short-term goals, and we can't do away with all the problems overnight. I think that remaining in that mindset and being realistic, while still being optimistic and ambitious, paves the way for you to continue activism and not feel like you're not doing enough and the world's not changing fast enough. That's very important, because I see activists who get heartbroken and burned out and beaten down, and instead of fueling their work more…it extinguishes their fire and they end up doing no activism.

"You know it took me a long time to realize that this is a trauma-related field. We talk so much about the abuse that the animals go through, which is absolutely true, but we have to acknowledge the fact that we're being faced with trauma on a daily basis.

"In some ways you have to separate yourself when you're watching the animal abuse videos, because if I were to become emotionally paralyzed every time I watched a video, I wouldn't be able to strategically think about what we need to do to address the abuses. Does it still affect me and do I still get heartbroken and upset about it? Yes, it does, of course, some cases more than others. But I really have learned to turn that emotion into a question: 'What is the plan and the strategy for addressing it?' When we have an investigation, and we get video back of horrific animal abuse, it's disturbing for me to see, but I quickly turn that anger into activism and action steps. We determine that we need to go to law enforcement, we need to file a criminal complaint, we need to get experts involved, we need to have a news conference, and we need to get this out to the public.

"We did an investigation in Texas where they were bashing in the skulls of cattle with pick axes and hammers to kill them—horrible, horrible abuse. In the work that we do, we see the darkest side of humanity, yet we also see the brightest side of humanity. We see the compassion that people have; we see the generosity that people have. Still, it's not as if they all even each other out."

Mercy for animals undercover video reveals sick and injured dairy cows
being killed by hammer blows to the skull.

As a bulwark against overwhelm, Nathan began practicing yoga. He purposely set out to make friends outside the animal protection movement. He is keenly aware of the need to explore outside interests, and to stay connected to the rest of the world outside his area of expertise.

"It's so easy to get wrapped up in a community, and you can lose perspective on the rest of society. From a purely effectiveness standpoint, we have to keep our feet grounded in reality, or else we're not going to be able to communicate with the rest of the population."

LEADERSHIP, REALISM, AND OPTIMISM

"You only need look through history to see the progress we've made on all sorts of issues in a relatively short amount of time in order to gain a positive outlook on human nature."

"I definitely consider myself a leader, and that's an important trait. Another primary asset one needs is dedication. Dedication is a word that's thrown around a lot for a lot of things, but as I mentioned, the dedication of working without another staff member for more than five years, and pushing forward and standing out in the cold, and all of those things really define dedication. Dedication also defines the unwavering belief that things are going to get better.

"I'm a realist, but I also think that I'm a realist with an optimistic outlook. I don't walk around the world sugar coating everything, but I do believe we can better many situations. You only need look through history to see the progress we've made on all sorts of issues in a relatively short amount of time in order to gain a positive outlook on human nature and its move towards a kinder, more encompassing, future.

"I often times talk about our generation and where we stand right now. We have two paths that we can go down: one is a very negative, destructive path, and this is not just with animals, but also with the environment as a whole. We could continue to increase meat consumption and factory farming, take factory farming to other countries where it didn't exist, and the amount of animal abuse increases. We can go down a path where we continue to overfish our oceans, and the fish population continues to decline. We can continue to pollute our environment, and global warming continues to increase. There are certainly signs that could be the path that we go down, and it's a very destructive path that will lead to water shortages and food shortages and climate change, further animal abuse, and all of that.

"Or, we can choose to go down a path where people start to wake up to these issues, and we start to use our human creativity and ingenuity to address the issues and become more efficient and more conscious in how we do things. I think there is a big trend and push in that direction.

"There is a growing public sentiment on these issues to make change. I have full confidence that as a human civilization we are capable of addressing these issues. But there must be a desire to address them, and a level of education and awareness, and it's going to come from constituents pushing for that, and corporations pushing for that, it's going to come from the legislative system pushing for that, which is why we have such a multipronged approach to what we do.

"Looking back now, I'm actually very grateful that my starting point was a rural town in Ohio, because if you can maintain those values and that lifestyle in that type of community and farm culture, you can do it anywhere. Now I live in West Hollywood, California, and it's like a walk in the park. I have 17 vegan restaurants within a mile of my home."

Living in Los Angeles has been good for Mercy for Animals as well, allowing Nathan and his staff to draw on animal-loving and environmentally-aware spokespeople from Hollywood, the media, music, and other fields to help raise funds. With such well-known names lending support of either their faces, voices, names, or money, Mercy for Animals is able to draw greater attention to its efforts to reduce animal suffering and increase compassion.

While Nathan started Mercy for Animals alone in a rural town in Ohio, it now has an international presence with MFA Canada firmly established, and undercover investigators working across the globe. As factory farming continues to expand further inside Mexico, China, India, and elsewhere, Nathan expects the future to be equally challenging.

Yet in a world where one person with a positive attitude, clear focus, and a desire for a more benevolent world can harness their own passion, inspire a movement, and assemble a team with the ability to influence hearts and minds the world over, it's a future with hope restored.

DR. RAED MUALEM
Nazareth Academic Institute

A BRIDGE TO PEACE: SECURING EDUCATION FOR ARAB YOUTH IN ISRAEL

"My community, Palestinian Christian and Muslim citizens of Israel, could be a bridge between Israel and the entire Arab world. We understand the Israeli narrative and we live the Arab culture and tradition—I believe we can be this bridge for peace between Israel and Arab nations."

For more than 40 years Arab community leaders living in Israel have been fighting an uphill battle on a muddy slope. Their goal of providing higher education to the minority Arab population in Israel has been a monumental undertaking rife with frustration and heartbreak. While Dr. Raed Mualem didn't start the race, he has painstakingly carried the torch through a volley of obstacles for nearly two decades, steadfastly refusing to let the fire go out.

Although educated at Oranim College and Tel Aviv University as a biology professor and researcher, Dr. Mualem has subjugated his love of science to focus his efforts on bringing world-class education to his people. To him, nothing could be more important to their future, nor to the effort of building peace in the Middle East.

Dr. Mualem and his family live in Nazareth, an Arab city located in the Galilee region of Israel where the majority of Palestinian citizens in the country live. Christians believe the province of Galilee is where Jesus lived and practiced his ministry and where he performed many miracles.

As a man bearing many identities—Palestinian, Arab, Christian, and Israeli, Raed floats easily between Israel's majority Jewish population and its minority Muslim and Christian Palestinian population. He teaches at a Jewish college to make ends meet. While his immediate goal is to educate his people, Palestinian citizens of Israel, his ultimate goal is using education to connect Arabs and Jews inside Israel, and eventually extend that process to the rest of the Middle East.

"My community, Palestinian Christian and Muslim citizens of Israel, could be a bridge between Israel and the entire Arab world. We understand the Israeli narrative and we live the Arab culture and tradition—so I believe we can be this bridge for peace between Israel and Arab nations."

His goal, however, requires a core building block that remains illusive: bringing higher education and critical thinking skills directly to the doorstep of his Palestinian community in Israel. It is an objective Raed has dedicated his working life to achieve. However, while many Jewish Israelis support his vision of bringing world-class education to Galilee, others do not. Thus, his battle to open an accredited and government-funded college for Arab youth, be they Christian or Muslim, has become an epic saga with as many twists and turns as the beleaguered peace process itself.

Raed Mualem will never give up his hope of building a peaceful Middle East—one in which every person is educated and every person is given equal opportunities regardless of his or her ethnic, national, or religious origins. This is his personal vision of creating peace.

AN UNLIKELY BEGINNING

"My parents told us the Jews had been through the Holocaust and we needed to share our land with them. This was the type of environment I grew up in. My mother and father told us, 'If you don't have forgiveness in your heart you will never overcome life's challenges.'"

Raed Mualem was born in the tiny village of Mi'ilya, the only remaining Christian village in Israel today, located north of Nazareth near the Lebanese border. The son of poor farmers with 4th grade educations, Raed says he learned survival, love, and forgiveness from his parents. When the state of Israel was proclaimed in 1948 on land known for centuries as Palestine, the new Israeli government seized the majority of his family's farmland.

"When this land was Palestine, my family owned and farmed 300 dunams (75 acres). After 1948 the new Israeli government confiscated 2/3 of our land, leaving us with only 100 dunams."

Raed knows that relative to the hundreds of thousands of Palestinians who remained refugees after the 1948 war, his family was fortunate to retain and live on a portion of their own land. Yet, despite their tragic loss of friends, family, and precious farmland, and the stress of living under martial law from 1948 to 1966, Raed's parents preached only love and forgiveness to their children, never hatred or revenge.

"My parents told us the Jews had been through the Holocaust and we needed to share our land with them. This was the type of environment I grew up in. My mother and father told us, 'If you don't have forgiveness in your heart you will never overcome life's challenges.'"

Still, this rough and dramatic upheaval of his parents' lives thirteen years before his birth in 1961 contributed to a childhood of extreme poverty. Raed, with his siblings and parents, shared a simple home with his uncle, aunt, and cousins. Electricity had not made it to their village even in the 1960's so they made do without refrigeration and without a kitchen. Raed remembers falling asleep and seeing a goat hanging from the ceiling above him, preserved only by salt. They ate meat once a week, excepting holidays like Easter, when they ate meat every day for a week. They shared this simple home with their animals, including camels, cows, goats and chickens, all of whom slept on a dirt floor just five stone steps below the same large room where the family slept and ate. The smell was often oppressive, but the animals' presence provided warmth in the winter.

Despite living in poverty, their lives were unusually rich in community and education. As one of the only remaining Christian villages at that time, Mi'ilya garnered the attention of Father Elias Chacour, a local Palestinian priest whom Raed would join forces with decades later in an effort to educate Arabs of Israel. Father Chacour, or *Abouna*, as Palestinians refer to priests, would eventually become Archbishop of Galilee. At the time, though, he was a young priest who cared deeply about educating youth and thus set up a library in the village center just ten meters from Raed's family's home. The local bishop also visited the library regularly to tell stories to the children in the village and read books to them, always encouraging them to learn to read. Those books and stories opened up the entire world to Raed, who went on to earn a doctorate and several masters degrees.

At the time, however, life was a constant struggle for mere existence. "We grew wheat, tobacco, and olives and sold them in town. The prices were very low but enough to sustain our family. We grew our own vegetables and fruit and our animals provided eggs and milk. We were self sustaining but desperately poor. We had no car nor money to buy anything."

Raed credits his current work ethic and tenacity to his upbringing. "An agricultural life taught me perseverance and hard work. At midnight, my father, uncle, brother, cousin, and I went to the fields to cut the tobacco leaves in the moonlight until 1:30 am. We returned and slept, and then at 5 a.m., I took the goats to the mountain by myself. At 7 a.m. I left for school. At noon we had a half-hour break and I would go home to take water to the goats. I returned to school to finish the day then went home and back to the mountain to bring the goats home. So you grow up knowing how to work, how to persevere. All the villages had the same culture. In the fall we harvested olives and produced olive oil. We had to study and we had to work very hard."

The city of Nazareth, where Dr. Mualem lives with his wife and sons, is an hour's drive south of Mi'ilya where his elderly parents still live. Raed remains deeply connected to their family land.

"So now, even though I am a professor, and I work so many hours a week trying to open a college and keep it open, I still go to my parents' land with my wife and children every weekend in September or October to bring in the olive harvest. It's hard work, but this is our tradition."

EDUCATION AS THE CORNERSTONE OF PEACE

"We spoke together about how to create peace—how to create commonality between people in the region."

Always a disciplined student, Raed attended college at Oranim, a primarily Jewish school where he earned a bachelor's degree. It was there he met a physiology professor named Amiram Shkolnik, a well-known scholar who helped build Oranim College and who also helped start Tel Aviv University. He would become Raed's lifetime mentor as Raed followed him to Tel Aviv University to study for his master's degrees, and ultimately, to earn his doctorate degree.

"Amiram Shkolnik was Jewish, and he became one of the most important people in my life. We used to talk all the time because I rode with him to

Tel Aviv and back to my village every week. We spoke together about how to create peace— how to create commonality between people in the region. He was born during Ottoman times, when this area was still known as Palestine, and he had a great deal of concern about the future.

"Amiram Shkolnik brought some of the best scientists in the world to my home because he knew our family very well. He brought David Robertshaw, a professor from Cornell, with whom I still work today. He brought professors from Duke University including the best physiologist in the world. They all came to our tiny village. I was so lucky to meet these people.

"I came from a poor Christian family who believed in love and forgiveness, inspired by priests who felt it was so important to be educated. So I was very lucky. And I was modeled peace by my parents and by my Jewish professor who has sadly since passed away. This is how I came to understand myself as a human bridge."

EARLY ATTEMPTS AT OPENING
A COLLEGE FOR ARABS

Without college for these Palestinian students, Raed Mualem cannot see how to build that peaceful bridge he envisions.

While Arab students have been able to apply for entrance to existing colleges for decades, several factors kept the vast majority from doing so—a trend that continues today. The reasons are many and varied, beginning with language. Even though Hebrew is the national language, many Palestinian Israelis still speak Arabic at home and learn best in that language.

Similarly, Israeli colleges follow the religious tradition and close on Saturday. Palestinian citizens, depending on whether they are Muslim or Christian, worship on Sunday or Friday. This becomes a greater problem during religious events that extend over time, such as Passover, Christmas, and Ramadan.

Financially and culturally, it is also difficult to travel far from one's own town or village to attend college, especially for poor or more conservative families who wish to study close to home. So the end result is that few Arabs in Israel attend college relative to their 21% representation in the population.

Beginning in the 1970's, the mayor of Nazareth and several Arab professors approached the educational committee of the Israeli parliament to request that a college be opened to serve the Arab population in the Galilee. At that time, the request was flat out rejected without discussion.

"They were very clear about it. The government did not want to foster Palestinian nationalism in Israel. So there was no political will to open such a college and the attempts of those early leaders failed entirely."

Twenty more tumultuous years passed. Some students, including Raed, crossed cultural barriers and attended primarily Jewish colleges in towns and cities far from their homes and even further from their culture. The great majority, however, did not, and the two populations remained largely divided.

Raed was working on his PhD in Tel Aviv in 1996 when violence erupted in nearby Jerusalem. Members of Hamas, a Palestinian resistance group based in Gaza, began sending suicide bombers to blow up public busses. Violence that started in Jerusalem soon spread to Tel Aviv where suicide bombers struck a shopping mall, killing 20 people and injuring 75.

No one was caught in the middle of the ensuing five-year violent struggle more than the Palestinian citizens of Israel. Their own people, refugees now living in Gaza and the West Bank, were at war with the country of Israel where they lived and held citizenship. Raed's family and other Arab Israeli citizens became victims of suspicion by both Israeli Jews in Israel and Palestinian refugees in the West Bank and Gaza. History had relegated the Palestinian citizens of Israel to a people with no clear identity, a marginalized voice, and no true allies.

Palestinian youth in Israel with enough resources and aspirations began finding their way to colleges in Europe, Russia, or to other Middle Eastern countries, and in 2016 they continue to do so. The expense is tremendous, but far more painful for parents is the fact that their sons and daughters often remain in those countries after graduation, believing they cannot find acceptance and employment in Israel. The process has contributed to the further depletion of the already-fragile Palestinian community in Israel, and hinders its future.

What troubles Dr. Mualem most, however, is that today the majority of Palestinian citizens of Israel do not attend college at all. Without college, he fears their community will decline, a situation that harms efforts at fostering peace or prosperity for everyone in Israel. Without college, and the high paying jobs associated with a higher degree, he fears hopelessness will replace achievement. Without college for these Palestinian students, Raed Mualem cannot see how to build that peaceful bridge he envisions.

TAKING MATTERS INTO THEIR OWN HANDS

"I told my colleagues it was our role to create opportunity for our community and not just to do research or publish articles."

During the period of violence and unrest that began in the late 1990's, Raed felt vulnerable and helpless as he saw division growing between Jewish and Palestinian citizens. He decided to find and use the power he did have. He gathered a group of 45 Arab PhD students from around the country to discuss how they could create opportunity for their people.

"We were so shaken by the violence and felt we had to do something. And we realized something more; we needed to prepare our own people for peace and talk with them about how important it is to live in a multicultural society. I saw that the percentage of Palestinian Israelis getting a higher education was low and frustration was high. I told my colleagues it was our role to create opportunity for our community and not just to do research or publish articles. We needed to find a way to make higher education available to our own people."

After completing his dissertation, Raed worked with Abouna Chacour to open Mar Elias Educational institutions in the Arab town of I'billin, located in Galilee. The campus provided high-level education for kindergarten through high school. Building on that success, their team opened a two-year technical school for the local Palestinian community. It wasn't yet a college, but it became a proving ground to demonstrate the need, desire, and intention among Arab leaders that they were serious about educating their population.

The technical school was an immediate success, training 700 Arab students a year in computer-related engineering. Raed assisted Abouna Chacour in developing the campus and eventually became Vice President of the Mar Elias Educational Institutions. Buoyed by the demand and their success, they opened a regional teachers center, which quickly became the largest in all of Israel. According to Israel's Minister of Education, it was also the most successful.

"We developed a strong system because we believed we could build, strengthen, and improve our Palestinian society in Israel through education."

Throughout this time, Raed's Jewish friend and mentor, Professor Amiram Shkolnik, was by his side supporting his efforts. When it came to opening an academic college, Raed again sought his counsel on where to begin. Amiram's experience founding Oranim College and helping launch Tel Aviv University was an invaluable asset.

"The team of 45 Christian and Muslim Arab doctors I had formed in 1996 became the *Committee for the Establishment of the First Arab College.* They came from across Israel, from Jerusalem, Haifa, and Tel Aviv, from cities, towns, and villages. Once I had helped create a technical college and a regional teacher's center and we had had such high interest and success, I knew the time to open a college was right because we had built credibility."

The *Arab Doctors* put together a detailed proposal to present to Israel's Council for Higher Education (CHE). Raed was ready with a plan to develop four programs: Communication, Chemistry, Speech Therapy, and Computer Science.

"I got that recommendation from Professor Trachtenberg, who had been my professor at Tel Aviv University. We didn't choose Business or Law or something like that; we wanted to take a science and technology approach with a high skill side because there was a need for such skills in the country.

"In 2000 I presented the project to the Israeli Council for Education and they appeared shocked. We had selected about 25 of the 45 PhD's to teach and I was prepared with all their CV's (curriculum vitaes) proving that we were more than capable of accomplishing our goal. In addition, I had several Jewish colleagues I had studied with in Tel Aviv who wanted to teach at our college. It would be known for multiculturalism.

"The head of the Budget and Planning Committee told us, 'You came at the right time because we are just beginning our planning for the next five years.' Then he said, 'I think the location should be in Nazareth,' which was what I wanted. I was elated! I had used a practical, educational path instead of the political path, and it seemed to be the right approach.

"The process required us to apply to become a branch campus of Tel Aviv University. We did that, but were turned down because of the location limits. So we applied as a branch campus of Haifa University, which did not have the same limits, and were turned down again by the Council for Education. It was then we suspected we had a political issue. We just didn't realize how big and intractable that political problem would turn out to be."

POLITICS, POLITICS, AND MORE POLITICS

"Though it was easy for them to say no to us, it was very hard for them to say no to the United States."

Raed began to realize that while they had supporters in the Council for Education who saw the need for and supported the idea of opening a college to serve the Arab Palestinian minority, they also seemed to have opponents who carried more influence. The head of the budget and planning committee, the man who told them their timing was perfect, suggested they strengthen their case by creating academic facts on the ground.

Though deeply discouraged, Raed focused on how to create these facts, but just days later a fortuitous event occurred. Father George St. Angelo, a frequent traveler to the Galilee from the United States, visited Abouna Chacour and Raed at the educational campus in I'billin. With him was his colleague, Lynn Youngblood, the provost of the University of Indianapolis. Raed explained the recent rejection by Israeli schools for Mar Elias to become a branch campus and the difficulties they were experiencing in opening a college for Arab students. He asked if the University of Indianapolis would consider opening a branch on their Mar Elias campus. The university had already set a precedent by opening a branch campus in Athens, Greece.

Their reaction was immediately positive. The provost returned to the United States and less than three weeks later returned to Nazareth with Dr. Mary Moore, Associate Provost for International Relations. They talked for two days straight, creating a vision of an "American Branch of the University of Indianapolis in Galilee."

In the next month five professors from the University of Indianapolis traveled to Israel, and together with Raed and other professors created a syllabus, which they then submitted to the North Central Association, the equivalent of Israel's Council for Higher Education in the United States. The approval for opening an American-accredited branch campus in the Galilee came in less than three months.

"It was a very active and intensive time; all of this happened between October 2000 and February 2001. In fewer than four months, we moved from first meeting them, to bringing a team, to creating a concept, and getting approval from the North Central Association. Our concept was to have world-class teaching in English—to be the first college in Israel to offer a Bachelor of Arts in English. My idea was to have The American University in Galilee similar to the American University in Beirut."

Still, before they could take action, they still had to win approval from Israel's Council for Higher Education (CHE).

"So we submitted the proposal to the CHE in Israel during March or April in 2001. We worked on that for two and a half *years* without approval. 'Correct A, Correct B, Correct C.' This and that, over and over. We no longer suspected it be a political issue; we now *knew* that it was."

Undeterred, Raed decided to make a trip to Washington D.C., since the University of Indianapolis had contact with U.S. Senator Richard Lugar, who in turn had contacts in the U.S. Embassy in Tel Aviv.

"I shared with him all the facts and asked for his help. Senator Lugar, along with the U.S. Ambassador to Israel, wrote a strong letter to the Israeli Minister of Education, saying 'Why is it that the North Central Association of the United States can pass this approval in a short time while it cannot pass your assessment [in two and a half years]? Something is wrong here.'"

Indiana Senator Lugar meeting with Dr. Mualem in his Washington, D.C., office.

Finally, in July 2003, with no answer from the CHE in sight, Raed and his team made a decision to take their case to the Israeli Supreme Court to demand that the CHE approve or disapprove their application to open a branch campus of the University of Indianapolis based on the rule of law.

"We had answered every question, won approval from North Central, and the time for an answer was over.

"When I informed the CHE we were going to appeal to the Israeli Supreme Court, I asked the question, 'Why can't we have the right to establish a multicultural institute with world-class teaching that was approved by one of the highest-level councils for education in the world and offer this opportunity to the people of Galilee?' We all knew the real question was, 'Why can't Palestinian citizens of Israel have a college in their city?'

"At nearly the same time we told the CHE we were taking our case to the Israeli supreme court, the CHE also received the letter from the U.S. Embassy and Senator Lugar.

"Though it was easy for them to say no to us, it was very hard for them to say no to the United States. Almost immediately, the CHE approved the plan for Mar Elias to be a branch campus of Indianapolis. Within three months we were able to recruit eighty students and open our doors. It felt like a miracle."

A NEW BEGINNING

"We focused more on educating girls, initially, because we understood their opportunity to study was extremely limited. Our community needed women to become educated, to help create good decision makers in the society."

"We were so exuberant, off and running to put everything in place. We adopted the American higher education model, offering liberal arts as part of the program as well as general education core. We included social inquiry, living in a multi-cultural society, interfaith religion, and peace studies. Finally, we taught in English rather than Arabic or Hebrew. That was a huge departure from the status quo in Israel. We focused on excellence. This is how we started.

"We discovered also that only 1% of the professors in Israel were Arab, which meant that many Arabs had managed to earn doctorate degrees but couldn't find work in Israel. So in addition to educating Arab students, the college would accomplish several other things: it would bring employment to many Arab PhD's, it would stop the flow of students going outside the country to study, and it would raise the economic status of our community in the Galilee, which had very low income and low economic opportunity.

"Another close Jewish friend, Professor Manuel Trajtenberg, who had been my economy professor at Tel Aviv University, had spoken to me about developing 'human capital' in our community. I trusted him, understanding that if Palestinians in Israel develop human capital, investors will come to Nazareth and the Galilee, invest and mobilize, and create employment opportunities.

"We focused more on educating girls, initially, because we understood their opportunity to study was extremely limited. Our community needed women to become educated to help create good decision makers in the society. Only 20% of women were working and we needed to find a way to change this. We decided to start by having a college open to all, but oriented to women, many of whom come from area villages and towns that are conservative. For these young women to attend college, it had to be close to their homes. I always felt that many more women needed to become educated at the highest levels as it uplifts the family both economically and socially, and helps the society overall."

FIRST SUCCESS

"Our model placed Peace Studies as a foundation of our curriculum; we had Arab and Jewish professors working together, all teaching in English. Our vision worked!"

The branch campus of the University of Indianapolis opened in 2003 in the Muslim and Christian town of I'billin, on the Mar Elias campus alongside the elementary, high school, technical school, and teachers center. The Arab students were elated.

"First of all, the Arab students were studying in their own college, celebrating their own holidays. They felt for the first time they are not only an ID number in the university but were treated as a brother or a sister. They appreciated that very much. They knew they were part of something much bigger than themselves; they were part of building the institution and the community. They became practiced in talking to all kinds of visitors, including those making religious pilgrimages to Galilee from around the world.

"We learned a great deal working with the U.S. educational system. For example, students in the U.S. are required to purchase one primary text for each course, and the professor uses that text, and sometimes more than one as the basis for the course. In Israel there is no required text so students are dependent on the professor. This makes it much more difficult to learn basic facts for the course. So we adopted the American model. We also added a summer session as they do in the States. We also added critical thinking skills. We adopted all of that from the American system and culture. Our model placed Peace Studies as a foundation of our curriculum; we had Arab and Jewish professors working together, all teaching in English. Our vision worked!"

THE ROLLER COASTER RIDE RESUMES

"We graduated 231 students through those three years. Then, after graduation in 2006, the Israeli government shut us down again. They said, 'No more international branch campuses allowed inside the country.'"

In 2006, the first class graduated with an American degree from the University of Indianapolis. 90% of those graduates found jobs in Israel. They had a strong education, spoke Arabic, Hebrew, and English, and developed strong skills including interpersonal relations and understanding of the multicultural system. They had spent a summer semester studying on the U.S. campus of the University of Indianapolis and built close relationships. Today some of those students are teachers; some are working in high tech; and some went on to graduate study. Raed knows their degree was absolutely critical to their success.

First graduating class of 2006, University of Indianapolis,
I'billin branch campus in the Galilee region of Israel.

"We graduated 231 students through those three years. Then, after graduation in 2006, the Israeli government shut us down again. They said, 'No more international branch campuses allowed inside the country.'

"Whoosh! It was such a blow to so many, both in Israel and the in the United States. There had been so much excitement about our program— among U.S. Senators and in the press. We had so many positive articles written about our students in the U.S. press, like *Arab Israeli Students in the Crossroads*. The Jewish Federation of Indianapolis was also very shocked and disappointed as they had been so supportive of all our efforts."

Upon learning the news of the closure, Senator Lugar, then a member of the U.S. Senate Committee on Foreign Relations, wrote a second letter to the Israeli Minister of Education.

The Honorable Yuli Tamir
Israeli Minister of Education
Tel Aviv, Israel

Dear Minister Tamir:

I have long been a proponent of international educational exchanges, supporting both increasing the number of foreign students studying in the United States and urging American students to experience all the cultural and intellectual benefits that accrue from studying abroad. As a former Rhodes Scholar, I know first-hand how one's life can be inexorably changed for the better by such an opportunity.

In order to facilitate the flow of American students to institutions of higher learning overseas, many U.S. universities partner with institutions abroad, and the University of Indianapolis is no different. As the former mayor of Indianapolis and current Senator from Indiana, I have had numerous occasions to work with this University and believe they are a top-flight institution. Given the need for Americans to understand better the situation in Israel, I was particularly pleased to hear that they have been partnering successfully with Mar Elias University since 2005.

However, I understand that the government of Israel has elected to terminate such educational partnerships and that Mar Elias has actively, yet unsuccessfully, sought accreditation since 1996. I have heard many positive comments about Mar Elias and hope that its accreditation situation can be resolved quickly to allow it to recruit additional students. Finally, I believe that terminating international university partnerships could be counter-productive given Israel's historic tradition of openness and educational and intellectual dialogues.

I would appreciate hearing from you soonest on both these matters.

Sincerely,

Richard G. Lugar
United States Senator

Despite his impassioned request, the Senator's letter did not have the effect of his earlier efforts. The college would remain closed.

STARTING OVER, AGAIN

"I really felt crazy because I believed we had failed our entire community and they would not have any access to education or to improving their lives."

Devastated by the news, Raed Mualem, his colleagues, and their board felt they had the proverbial rug pulled out from under them. They had created such enthusiasm in their community, providing a tangible goal for high school students who knew they finally had a college they could attend. Without warning, their dreams for attending college lay shattered.

The closure was also a blow to the Jewish and Arab professors who taught at the college. They had sacrificed pay and sometimes reputation to leave their positions at high-ranking colleges and universities elsewhere in Israel to teach in this small town in Galilee. They shared the dream of building a multicultural, peaceful future for Israel, and now they had little to show for the risks they took and the efforts they made.

The only way to keep any semblance of a school open was for Mar Elias to apply to become a fully accredited college on its own. So they applied again, and for the following two years did everything in their power to appeal to the CHE for accreditation.

Abouna Chacour, who first opened Mar Elias Campus with a kindergarten built on land he purchased himself, became frustrated with the college effort because he could see that the CHE was blocking their every move. The elementary school, meanwhile, had expanded. There was no space on the campus for the fledgling college with no accreditation, no state funding, and no future.

"One day Abouna told me, 'Raed, it's not going to happen.' He said I was wasting time and money and I needed to accept that it's over."

Abouna Chacour fired Raed and the remaining staff in 2008, seeking to end the seemingly hopeless effort to continue working to resuscitate a college that showed no signs of life. Raed was devastated.

"It was a very hard time for me in June, 2008. I had no job, no money, and no idea of my future. I really felt crazy because I believed we had failed our entire community and they would not have any access to education or to improving their lives. It was about our struggle as a minority community— and I had failed them."

A man of constant action, Raed didn't spend long mourning. He contacted Susan Drinan, the Chair of their international board of directors for the school. The board had been the only source of income for students' tuition, raising money primarily from Americans who believed in the mission.

"The board in the U.S. did not give up on me. Neither did my family. I got the approval of my wife and children to take a loan to live on as I continued to fight. It was a difficult time to get a loan and to keep going for an entire year without any salary. But I just couldn't give up."

So, they began once again. Raed and his colleagues established a new NGO—Nazareth Academic Association—and named a businessman from Nazareth, Bishara Kattof, to chair its board. Kattof was a man who could easily communicate with the mayor of Nazareth and he was a go-getter who could make things happen. He did not disappoint.

Kattof asked Nazareth's mayor, Ramiz Jaraisy, if the municipality would be willing to supply land or resources if they moved the startup college to their city. The response was an enthusiastic, "Yes!" The city would provide classrooms in a local high school, and when the college received formal government accreditation, the city of Nazareth would also provide seventy dunams (17 acres) of land to build a campus.

A new name was chosen, one that represented a secular, multi-ethnic approach. Nazareth Academic Institute, or NAI, was born. Arab and Jewish professors were hired, students were recruited, and classes began in the local high school in space cordoned off for the college.

Raed and his colleagues dove head first into the process of applying once again to become a fully accredited, stand-alone Israeli college. Again they jumped through every hoop the CHE put before them.

"The process was hugely complex, slow, and chockfull of obstacles. We answered every challenge and roadblock put forth to us, both academically and politically."

STILL A LAND OF MIRACLES

"Condoleezza Rice contacted the U.S. Ambassador in Israel, who in turn contacted the Council for Higher Education (CHE), saying that this project, our school, was in the U.S. interest. This was a significant letter."

Raed trusts that if one believes in their vision so fully that he or she will risk everything to achieve it, then either through pure force of will or by a seemingly miraculous occurrence, they will achieve it. Not long after losing his job, being fired by his mentor, and taking a loan to support his family to continue his fight, that miracle happened.

"It happened that President Bush and Condoleezza Rice visited Israel, and as Christians, wanted to visit Nazareth and its many holy sites. I was fortunate to have the opportunity to meet them and share our vision for a multicultural university. I also shared our frustrations at not being accredited. They listened very intently, and afterwards, Condoleezza Rice contacted the U.S. Ambassador in Israel, who in turn contacted the Council for Higher Education (CHE), saying that this project, our school, was in the U.S. interest. This was a significant letter."

One year later, on March 29, 2009, Raed received the news from outgoing Israeli Prime Minister, Ehud Olmert, that the Cabinet approved the Council for Higher Education's decision to issue a permit to open an institute of higher education in the Arab sector. NAI was now fully accredited as an Israeli college.

Abouna Chacour (lower left), President George Bush, Condoleezza Rice,
Dr. Raed Mualem (upper right), local nuns, and others join hands at
Mount of Beatitudes in the Galilee region.

The news kept getting better. A Palestinian benefactor from the West Bank, billionaire businessman and philanthropist Munib al-Musri, announced he would donate the necessary money to the Nazareth Fund to build a physical campus in Nazareth. To have Mr. Al-Masri financially supporting their efforts was a game changer, one that seemed likely to complete the mission.

The creation of the Nazareth Fund was also a significant step forward. It became an engine for Arab citizens to invest in their own community. It was the first time the local community supported the establishment of a higher institution of learning. Not only did it supply funding from the community, it showed that it was no longer a handful of academics behind the effort to bring a college or university to the region, but an entire city and community. The momentum was undeniable.

Raed began to broaden his vision. They would establish a pre-med study program with Cornell University. They would offer a graduate degree in Peace Studies with Northwestern University, and possibly a program with Georgetown University for leadership. They began exploring an MBA program.

At the time Raed announced: "In 50 years we will be the largest university in the Middle East. High tech, high quality—this is how we create Middle

East leadership. The American University in Beirut has had a huge impact. We want an American style university in the Galilee. We will have trans-national higher education—this is the future! Even in the United States they don't realize that today you have to supply skills to kids that include global education, or you have nothing."

Nazareth Academic Institute began offering something very different from the usual Israeli approach—liberal arts in addition to the primary focus of study.

"When I was in college I studied only biology— nothing else! So NAI required 25% of our curriculum in liberal arts with a mandatory core that included: *Living in a Multicultural Society, Global Problems, Conflict Resolution and Conflict Management, Interfaith Studies, Peace Studies, and English, Hebrew, and Arabic*—subjects that are practical for these students. We need to keep our dream. Our theme is: Excellence, Globalization, Multiculturalism, and Service to the Community."

Shimon Peres, the Israeli President at the time, believed deeply in what NAI was doing. He talked about NAI in a speech, saying, "You Arabs in Israel can be the bridge to the Arab world. If 30% of our doctors in Israel are Arab, and we trust them, and we put our lives in their hands, we can make peace with the Arab community."

THE NEXT BATTLE BEGINS

Angry about bias in the educational system, his professor encouraged the Office for Economic Development, OECD, of which he was a member, to make a site visit to Nazareth.

As wonderful as receiving accreditation was, it wasn't long before the crushing news arrived that although they were accredited, they would not be eligible for government funding. This, despite the fact that out of the seven colleges located in the Galilee, the other six colleges, all located in Jewish municipalities, were government funded.

During this period, Raed discovered he needed additional skills to manage what was turning out to be a very long, uphill battle to get accreditation and funding. Though he had a doctorate in biology, he returned to Tel Aviv University to study Educational Management and Leadership in 2009. He was taking the class at the time the funding denial occurred. One of his professors came to his assistance. Angry about bias in the educational system, his professor encouraged the Organisation for Economic Co-operation and Development, OECD, of which he was a member, to make a site visit to Nazareth.

The OECD is a powerful international organization to which highly developed or highly developing countries desire membership. Israel, along with the United States and most Western European countries, are active members. The OECD sets up standards of equality as reflected in opportunity, education, and investment of its member countries throughout their populations and highlight issues of inequality where it finds them.

As Israel's new Prime Minister, Benjamin Netanyahu sought membership in the prestigious organization. However, it became obvious to the OECD team that first visited I'billin, and later, Nazareth, that equality was nowhere to be found when it came to higher-educational opportunities for the Palestinian population inside Israel's borders.

Raed's Jewish professor was deeply troubled by the situation Arabs in Israel were facing in educational discrimination. As a working member of the OECD, he arranged for the organization to invite Raed to make a presentation at the *OECD Roundtable Meeting on Higher Education and Regional and City Development* in Paris. It was the opportunity for Raed to make his case to the international community.

Raed prepared and prepared more, creating a presentation that reflected statistical facts as well as the human toll. In July of 2010, Raed made his case before an international body. As he underlined the situation and the potential impact Nazareth Academic Institute would have on human capital development and on economic and social development of the Galilee region, they listened with rapt attention and agreed to look into the situation further.

After conducting their own thorough research, the OECD presented a scathing 200-page report to the Israeli government, as well as to all OECD countries. It clearly spelled out the entire untenable situation, citing such statistics as these: Although Arab citizens made up more than 20% of the Israeli population, only .7% of academic staff in the country were Arab, only 9% of students pursuing higher education were Arab, 6000-8000 Arab students were traveling to Jordan to study, and 54% of Arabs lived in poverty. How, therefore, could the Israeli government deny Arab college funding?

Because membership in the OECD was, and remains, critically important to Israel's leadership, and because the 200-page negative report was so thoroughly an indictment of the inequality that Palestinian citizens of Israel face, Raed and his colleagues expected a dramatic announcement.

Despite the OECD reports, and the fact that Israel is a member of the OECD, the requests for funding went unanswered. NAI limped along for the next three years as Raed traveled around the world trying to raise funds with the international board of trustees. The campus land was still available, the promise of funds to build the buildings was still intact, but the funding for daily operations, including money to pay a teaching staff, never came. They stayed afloat, just barely, with donations that the board in the U.S. was able to raise, and from the local Arab members of the Nazareth Academic Association. Raed continued to teach part time at a Jewish college.

Professors who believed in the mission, both Jewish and Arab, worked for little or no pay. Students paid what their families could afford, and the college hobbled along despite frequent and intermittent closings by the CHE for one reason or another.

THE FINAL MIRACLE?

"Let me share my dream with you."

At 6 o'clock p.m. in the summer of 2013, Raed was laboring in his office to secure any semblance of funding that might keep their floundering college open for another month. A man of incredible focus, it took some effort to draw his attention from his work and notice the two men standing in the main office looking around with apparent interest. Jumping to his feet, Raed offered his hand to welcome the strangers, one of whom had a decidedly American air about him.

"Hello, I am the provost of Texas A&M University in the U.S. I am in Israel scouting locations for a new branch campus for our school. I heard about your efforts to open a college here in Nazareth, and I'd like to learn more."

Raed's serious expression gave way to a broad smile, as he saw another chapter in their saga open before him in that very moment.

"Let me share my dream with you," Raed told him.

Share his dream, he did, in a powerful manner. Four months later, the entire world shifted for Raed and his colleagues at NAI. Rick Perry, the governor of Texas, arrived in Israel to sign an agreement with Israel's President, Shimon Peres, to open a branch campus of Texas A&M in conjunction with NAI. All were assured the law to accept a branch campus would be amended to allow this game-changing opportunity.

Not only would the Palestinian Arab citizens of Israel have access to the world-class education Raed had worked for, they would have masters and doctoral programs and research facilities. The financial boom to the community would be unparalleled. It almost seemed too good to be true.

Texas Governor Rick Perry points at Dr. Raed Mualem,
while then Israeli President Shimon Peres smiles broadly in the forefront.

And yet, despite the very public celebration and international coverage, more than two and a half years have passed since that ceremonial signing event— two and a half years that have resulted in delays, roadblocks, and more dead ends. Texas A&M, with all of its millions of dollars to invest, has been stymied in their efforts to support changing "relevant governing policy" that prevents branch campuses from operating in Israel, though they had been assured at the outset the policy would be changed.

SUCCESS ARRIVES WITH A POSITIVE, YET STILL UNCLEAR—OUTCOME

"Mr. Trajtenberg led in a powerful way to fight for us—to fight for justice. He convinced the rest of the planning committee to approve funding for an Arab college. He has ethical power. He has transformative leadership."

Mazen Qupty, Raed's colleague and friend, serves as NAI's representing attorney and chairman of the board. He has been fighting in the trenches in every possible way to secure funding and to move the Texas A&M partnership forward. In that role, he was the first to receive the news.

On November 18, 2014, Israel's Council for Higher Education at very long last, stated, "There is justification for the existence of a budgeted, general academic campus in an Arab town in northern Israel."

While it didn't name NAI specifically, to Raed, no words could have been sweeter, nor more promising. Government funding for a college serving Arab students was always the light at the end of the painfully long tunnel. It was the change he had long awaited and worked for.

Raed understands exactly how and why the CHE or Council finally approved funding for an Arab college. It goes back to his belief in building solid and long-standing relationships. Back in the nineties, when Raed was working on his doctorate, he took the advice of his professor and mentor, Professor Trajtenberg, at the University of Tel Aviv who had once counseled Raed to focus on building up so-called "human capital" in the Arab sector.

In the end, it was Professor Trajtenberg, a Harvard-educated Israeli, who ended up in the highly influential position as head of Budget and Planning for the CHE. He knew Raed's long story and the history of the Arab community's efforts for almost 20 years. He was now in the position to make change.

"Mr. Trajtenberg led in a powerful way to fight for us—to fight for justice. He convinced the rest of the planning committee to approve funding for an Arab college. He has ethical power. He has transformative leadership."

While the funding announcement is the highest victory Raed sought these many years, NAI still must take additional steps to be *the* college that receives the funding. As of June, 2016, applications are being reviewed for colleges who wish to provide this higher education for Arab students, and that includes existing colleges in Israel who may want to open a campus in the Galilee region serving the Arab community.

To be as competitive as possible, NAI co-applied for funding with Bar Ilan University, Israel's second-largest academic institution. If approved, the two schools will work together to offer a wide variety of courses with high-academic offerings in the city of Nazareth.

Should this partnership receive the highly sought-after funds, Raed Mualem and his colleagues can still look forward to the future involvement of their friends at Texas A&M, whose Provost recently expressed her pleasure at the news of "an emerging partnership between Bar Ilan University and the Nazareth Academic Institute," and wrote that they look forward to "exploring possible ways by which Texas A&M University faculty, students, and staff may benefit from this learning opportunity in Nazareth."

One thing is certain. Opportunity for Palestinian Arab students in Israel to study at an institution of higher learning will greatly expand in 2016.

So with a future full of promise, Raed Mualem visibly relaxes just a bit for the first time in more than sixteen years. Maybe twenty. He smiles more easily than he has in years.

Regardless of whether it is NAI/Bar Ilan or another school who receives the funding, the city of Nazareth will transform as more and more of its youth attend college and as new businesses pursue opportunities. The city, now desperate for improvements in infrastructure and municipal services, will flourish. As youth begin to believe in their own futures, and the value of their own voices, there is no telling what achievements will blossom.

But of course, Raed dreams that NAI will be the school selected to enjoy the funding he has long fought for.

PERSONAL CHARACTERISTICS NEEDED TO KEEP THE VISION GOING

"When you don't see the light of hope yourself, you must create the light."

After sixteen years of continuous hard work, and with resolution ever closer, Raed believes the difference between potential success and ultimate failure comes down to personal strengths of focus, determination, inspiration, flexibility, and a solid, immutable belief in one's mission.

"Determination is key if you want to make change in the world," Raed says. "You cannot make a difference unless you realize that you need to absorb challenges and see that challenge as an opportunity for improvement. What I have learned is that you have to become assertive. Sometimes you have to learn what is yes, what is no, what is cold, what is hot. These past sixteen years, even with the determination, the forgiveness, and the endless hard work, it comes to a point where if people think you are weak, you cannot succeed. So these challenges change your life—change your mentality. You have to let them know that you are not weak.

"I have also learned to inspire others. It is important to show others that they need to take charge and lead their communities, and to keep going even when others think it's time to give up. At one point in 2011, many friends and colleagues told me, 'It's time to shut down. It's clear we are not going to be funded by the State of Israel.'

"Because we had worked for eleven years and became accredited, they thought we had tried everything. I said, 'What? Shut down? We are going to be funded. You have to believe in that.'

"So I had to keep hope alive. People need to see the light. Without that, they will be disappointed and give up. And when you don't see the light of hope yourself, you must create the light. You challenge yourself. You challenge your community. This is what it is all about.

"I was a biologist—but I had to become a politician, a leader, a business-man—all the things I was not. I had to study them to learn how to do them. All the time I am learning. You need to educate yourself; develop the skills.

"But the most important thing to consider before you ever start to act is this: You must believe *completely* in what you are doing. If you do, and you have the faith, and you know you will face challenges, they will never shake your faith in your mission. From day one I knew that we were going to make this happen. I knew it might take 10 or even 15 years. It's taken 16 so far. So what? You must put all your energy in that end goal and keep your eye on your vision. Every challenge you meet should be an opportunity to improve and move you closer to your goal. If you do not believe in that, and have faith in that, you will not succeed."

DR. BERNARD AMADEI
Founder, Engineers Without Borders USA

ENGINEERING TO REDUCE POVERTY

"Improving the lives of the 5 billion people whose main concern is to stay alive by the end of each day on our planet is no longer an option for engineers; it is an obligation."

As Dr. Bernard Amadei wandered through the dense landscape, a young girl in the distance drew his attention. No more than ten years of age, she was crouched beside a river, filling a large water vessel she steadied with tiny hands. Then, staggering under its weight, she lifted the heavy pot and placed it atop her head, balancing and supporting it with two reed-thin arms. He watched as she began making her way from the river back toward her village, her bare feet carefully plodding across the jungle floor, her eyes focused solely on the trail ahead.

It was a watershed moment for Dr. Amadei. He would soon learn that all of the girls in this village of San Pablo, and many of the boys, never attended school, their young lives obliged to jobs that ensured the survival of the 950 Mayan Indians living in the heart of the Belize jungle.

San Pablo's plight weighed heavily on him. It was a community entrenched in poverty, with scarce food, meager opportunities, and no plan or pathway to change. Emotionally impacted by their struggle and knowing he possessed the ability to help, Dr. Amadei set out to analyze how his engineering skills might somehow improve their chances for living healthier, and hopefully, more satisfying lives.

The actions he took next would not only improve life for that young child and her village—they would be the first steps toward building a movement, one that would ultimately transform and uplift the lives of millions of people living in crippling poverty around the globe.

However, such grandiosity was not Bernard Amadei's style; such thoughts did not even cross his mind.

There is an ancient yoga principle that suggests the less one strives to achieve something, the easier and more likely it will manifest. This may account for the enormous impact Dr. Amadei made in record time, with no clear intent to do so.

His goal was never to change the face of engineering, nor subsequently, engineering education. Nor was it to improve the lives of more than 2.5 million people in 45 countries across the world, from Moldova to Peru, from Malawi to Macedonia, from Togo to El Salvador. He wanted only to enable that ten-year-old Mayan girl in the jungle of Belize to go to school.

However, as the French poet Victor Hugo once said, "Nothing is stronger than an idea whose time has come."

DESTINY BECKONS

"For the first time in my life, there was a convergence between my engineering skills and my deep desire to be of service."

The story began with a seemingly fortuitous event, although Bernard Amadei does not believe in accidents. In 1997, he and his family bought a house in Lafayette, Colorado, near the University of Colorado where he teaches engineering. Dr. Amadei hired a company to landscape his new yard, an action he says forever changed his life.

Three men in their thirties showed up, ready to work. They came from Belize, a country in Central America Dr. Amadei had not heard of before. Intrigued by his gap in knowledge, he peppered the young men with questions about their lives and their country, and his good nature and sincerity prompted them to open up about their own hardships. He listened intently as they recalled the harsh conditions of life in Belize, formerly known as British Honduras.

Yet, as oppressive as their own destitution had been, Bernard discovered the young men's greatest concern was not for themselves; rather, they spoke emotionally about the needs of Mayan natives, telling a story of desperate poverty and hopelessness for the indigenous people of Belize.

When the focus of the conversation shifted to Dr. Amadei, he told them of his career in engineering and the position he held as a professor at the university. One of the men asked Dr. Amadei if he would consider visiting

Belize to provide Mayan Indians with hands-on, vocational training that could help improve their lives. Deeply moved by their story, he thought about it only briefly before agreeing to do what he could, when he could.

Helping people is in Dr. Amadei's blood. Before the rigors of academia took hold, he volunteered often, once as an intake associate at a homeless shelter for seven years. So this new request from the landscapers felt right to him, and he was eager to help.

Despite his willingness, two years passed before he heard from them again, and the conversation they'd had eventually faded into the recesses of his memory. Then, one day an email arrived from Angel Tzec, one of the landscapers who had returned to live in Belize.

"Please, if you can, I am still interested in having you come to Belize, and see what you can do to help these young Mayans."

When the time for his sabbatical arrived, Dr. Amadei seized the opportunity to visit Belize. Led by Angel, who was by then representing the Belize Ministry of Agriculture, Bernard traveled from one Mayan village to the next, assessing the situation, taking notes, and absorbing every bit of information he could. All of which led him to the village of San Pablo, and to the young girl carrying the water pot with no time to attend school.

Angel asked Dr. Amadei if he could install a pump to transport water from the river to the village. Bernard noted there was no electricity to power a pump, and it seemed likely there was no money available to provide fuel. As water technology was not his area of expertise, Dr. Amadei consulted his colleagues back at the university to seek a workable solution. They did not let him down, suggesting he look at a 200-year old technology that might provide an answer.

For Bernard Amadei, everything suddenly felt right.

"For the first time in my life, there was a convergence between my engineering skills, and my deep desire to be of service."

Dr. Amadei visiting with children at an EWB-US project in East Africa.

DISCOVERING A NEW WAY TO ENGINEER

"The idea came at the right time, at the right place, and we were the right people. That was the tipping point".

Upon returning to teaching at the end of his sabbatical, Dr. Bernard told his students about the project in Belize and asked if anyone might be interested in working on it with him. Suddenly it seemed as if he had woken a sleeping giant, tapping into a latent desire among youth to use their knowledge and skills to make the world better.

"It had nothing to do with the class they were taking, but they were very excited about the project: first two, then five, then ten students came forward. Eventually we put together a team of fourteen, and with the help of a technician friend of mine, I began to understand exactly what we would need."

While still in Belize, Bernard had learned of a waterfall in the jungle a scant quarter-mile from the village of San Pablo. The waterfall could provide kinetic energy that could be converted to pressure energy. His colleagues suggested he install a pump at the head of the waterfall, which could power the transport of water the distance to the village.

They raised $14,000 from various individuals to fund the project, and with a prototype in hand, he returned to Belize with the team of engineering students and installed the pump.

"It was a powerful experience and the students' excitement was uncontainable. They told me they wanted a more meaningful type of engineering education. I understood them. The traditional process can be boring. They told me they were tired of doing questions at the end of chapter five, and I was tired of grading questions at the end of chapter five. So we brought real life learning into their education, and it became our model."

After the trip, everything changed. "The idea came at the right time, at the right place, and we were the right people. That was the tipping point. I will always remember the day a student came to me and said, 'We have to start an organization. We got so much out of that project, we have to start something to keep it going.' And I said, 'No, no... don't drag me into something else. I have enough with my publishing and teaching.'"

"But of course, we started Engineers Without Borders in the United States. Fourteen years later, we have over 16,000 members."

A NEW TAKE ON AN OLD PROBLEM

"We are doing projects right, from an engineering point of view, but also doing the right projects, from a human point of view."

The Engineers Without Borders model was originally conceived in Amadei's home country of France as a small, student-run organization, *Ingénieurs Sans Frontières*. Dr. Amadei envisioned his American effort a bit differently. When structuring Engineers Without Borders-USA, he steered away from the traditional student-led movement, deciding that EWB-USA would be a professional, non-profit organization.

"I describe it as a non-profit engineering company. Whether working here in the developed world or in the developing world, we have the same quality control, the same quality assurance. We are doing projects right from an engineering point of view, but also doing the right projects from a human point of view. We take a sustainable point of view that is respectful of cultures, and also respectful of people's needs."

The project in Belize served as the model, yet it provided a shaky start, as it proved to be far more challenging than Bernard Amadei or anyone else anticipated. Once the equipment was installed and working, it wasn't long before a large flood occurred and the pump failed. The group had to return to Belize many, many times.

"My colleague, Denis, arranged to drill a well at the top of the village, and later, another EWB group installed a solar pump. So it was a door that opened up projects for other groups, and it made me realize that, number one, there was a lot of excitement among the students, which we needed to tap into because that doesn't happen very often. And two, there was a whole new field of engineering emerging for the developing world; engineering for poverty reduction. I looked around and no one was doing that work, which I found interesting. This is true, even though you have five billion un-served and under-served people on this planet."

Dr. Amadei realized that traditional engineering was geared to serve a fraction of the people on the planet; those living almost exclusively in richer, more developed countries. And while the principles of engineering are the same everywhere, the implementation in poor and undeveloped countries is quite different.

"That means you have to introduce failure into your design. Failure in the sense that you install something in a culture that is different, where the habits are different, where the income is less than a dollar a day, and the maintenance and operation of that technology is going to be quite different than what it is in Boulder, Colorado."

As EWB-US gathered speed, direction, and enthusiasm, Dr. Amadei discovered a new problem; virtually no engineers had been trained to do the types of projects desperately needed in developing countries. With nearly half of the world's 7.3 billion people living on less than $2.50 a day, there was no problem uncovering the limitless need for help; the problem was a lack of people trained to do the work.

To address that gaping disparity, in 2003 Bernard Amadei launched *Engineering for Developing Communities,* an educational program offering masters and doctorates at CU Boulder. Working in partnership with Engineers Without Borders-USA, the center would train engineers to focus on communities where people were living on less than $2.50 a day. Six years later, in 2009, the program received a $5 million dollar endowment from the Mortenson Family, owners of a large, local construction company, and was renamed The *Mortenson Center in Engineering for Developing Countries.*

Once the Mortenson Center opened, something interesting happened: more and more students who applied to study at the new center were women—far more than half. And the rising number of women in the engineering program at CU since then was another unexpected outcome Dr. Amadei didn't plan or anticipate.

"Engineering is about people to start with; it's not just about math and equations. We discovered a need for creating a new form of engineering practice and education to tap into that desire to help people—something we have been seeing more and more in young people. The students who come to the Mortenson Center are top-notch students."

A CU engineering student cutting rebar at a project in Peru.

Engineering is often seen as a dull control of nature. Although it's often presented that way, Bernard Amadei doesn't believe that's the way it should be taught. This new human focus of engineering brings people and cultures into the discussion. It is the type of engineering that requires a commitment from the heart and from the mind.

"There is a very strong engineering component in our work because it is about water; it is about sanitation, it is about shelter, and it is about education. At its core, however, it is about improving the lives of people. It's not engineering that happens in the top two inches of your head. It's engineering that requires the whole person, which we haven't dared to talk about in school, to discuss the compassionate or the human aspect of engineering."

Today Dr. Amadei refers to this work as *Engineering for the Other Ninety Percent*. In a TED talk, he said:

> "It's not just about technology—it's about public health, it is about social entrepreneurship, it is about dignity, it is about policy, it is about governance. And it's about appropriate technology—long lasting, owned by the people, understood by the people, that can be fixed by the people. It's a technology that creates jobs in a respectful way—respectful to nature, respectful to human beings, respectful to the environment. It's technology with a human face."

THE DARK SIDE OF GIVING ALL

"My wife can tell you that for six months I was not functioning."

Nature abhors a vacuum, and the lack of engineering programs serving the billions of people living in poverty was just that. When Dr. Amadei discovered this void, and created a way to fill it, the rush of people and projects that followed was quite literally overwhelming. New chapters popped up across the country so quickly they could scarcely keep up with the pace. Those chapters were discovering needed engineering projects worldwide.

Dr. Amadei devoted every free minute of his time and every ounce of his energy to the development of Engineers without Borders-USA and to the development of the Mortenson Center. Yet, he was still teaching a full load of engineering courses and maintaining a rigorous research practice, as the world of the universities continues to be one of publish or perish. His workload was staggering. After their first project in San Pablo was complete, and water started flowing into the village, people there started asking for energy.

"To be frank, I got very scared. I did not know what would come next. We finally passed the Belize project to the Colorado School of Mines, and then another project came in Mali, and another in Mauritania, and very quickly the projects grew and grew, and I was the only conductor! I didn't even have the ability to follow the final outcome of the first village."

For the following five years Dr. Amadei continued to manage the programs and juggle his teaching, research, and projects. By 2006, the toll came due. He became physically sick and emotionally overwrought.

"People have to realize this is not always a rosy path. It is very disturbing to the status quo, which of course is the point. But eventually the healer has to be healed. So yes, you want to change the world; yes, you want to make the world a better place, you want to do something that is sustainable. At the same time, how do you sustain yourself? This idea of giving and receiving is important to look at. Giving can actually draw a lot of energy out of you. It is most draining if you don't know how to receive, and if you don't know how to take care of yourself."

Fortunately, Dr. Amadei is happily married and the father of two children. His family's support helped sustain him through a very dark period. Yet at times he felt he had nothing left to give them either.

"My wife can tell you that for six months I was not functioning. That was when help came from various colleagues. The current executive director of EWB-USA, Cathy Leslie, came forward and said, 'I am a project manager. I can take care of it.' Now she is fully employed as the executive director and doing a fantastic job. Then Robyn Sandekian became the managing director of the Mortenson Center. So I was able to recoup and rejoin a more sane type of environment."

What can someone with a dream to change the world take away from his experience? Bernard Amadei believes one must take a clear and unfettered look at their grand idea to improve the world, and make sure they are ready to take that first step; considering their own situation, their goals, the strength of their passion, and the depth of their resources, their support system, and their willingness to engage.

"So this idea of a person having a vision of changing the world and every-one is dancing…I don't believe in that. It was painful at many levels; physically, psychologically, and at the soul level. Someone comes up with a great idea, and the universe essentially converges on that person and says. 'This is great, the world is going to be a better place,' and everyone has a great experience. However, that's not necessarily true. My experience was far from that. For me it was painful to give birth to an organization that had a very strong organic growth to it. I'm glad other people have taken the lead in supporting the organization. I see myself more as a scout … someone who makes new tracks in the forest and doesn't look behind. If people want to follow, they follow. If they don't want to follow, that's up to them."

However, when he steps back mentally and emotionally from the topic, even briefly, he remembers the upside of all that transpired.

"I don't want to say that the experience of starting EWB-USA was negative. It was rewarding. Opening new trails is fun. It creates new opportunities. It makes the world a better place. In our case it created a form of engagement for the engineering world that was not there before. And it needed some fresh awakening."

Which brings us to a second perspective. Dr. Amadei admits that perhaps, after all, it may have been better that he didn't know the difficult side of things, or he may not have done something he believes needed to be done.

"Ignorance is bliss to a certain extent. At the beginning there is so much energy in the heart that drives the effort, and that has to go somewhere.

When combined with the head, it has a very transformative type of power. It's not just compassion. It's not just 'doing good'. It's compassion in action."

"I know there aren't many organizations that jump from ten people to 16,000 people in fourteen years; so I know something significant happened. And many young engineers have been dramatically impacted; they transformed from feeling dull to becoming alive!"

THE CHALLENGE OF PASSION

"There is a joy in making the world better—but the pain associated with it— the birthing—can tear you apart. You have to be ready."

Passion is the foundation of any great endeavor. Without it we lose interest and energy. With it, we can accomplish seemingly superhuman feats. Dr. Amadei is a fascinating mix of practicality and unbridled passion, which together created an unstoppable force so powerful he was not able to control it himself.

"To make real change, one person must have a vision, and they must transmute it into action. If you want to change the world, you must bring your passion, heart and mind into your work. That's how transformation happens."

Being deeply introspective and spiritual, he has given the process years of reflection and analysis. The process has given rise to more questions, and they are questions for which he very much wants to find answers.

"Passion is an asset and a curse. It's a double-edged sword. The fire in the heart has a mind of its own. How do you capture that, and who is providing you guidance? Passion puts more and more fuel on the fire, and fire can eat you up completely if you aren't careful. In making the world a better place, how do you retain balance? How does one be still and not get caught in the passion?"

CU Boulder Engineers without Borders students in Kigali, Rwanda.

Dr. Amadei puts forth an important question. "Ultimately, is there a model out there that would allow someone to do these things, even bigger things, and remain sane? What are the prerequisites for someone who has a great vision? Perhaps before putting that vision into practice, one may want to develop a spiritual practice. My religion is compassion. Right now I am studying the Sufi tradition. I have had many good discussions with spiritual mentors, and others on the road to understanding. These are people who are also on the path and still asking questions."

'There is a joy in making the world better—but the pain associated with it—the birthing—can tear you apart. You have to be ready. Prepare yourself."

Going forward, Dr. Amadei wants to ask what the guidelines might be for those who want to do something big to affect change in the world. The fact is, he still doesn't know those answers. He suggests that perhaps there are no guidelines; maybe one must simply make them up as they go.

Clearly Dr. Amadei's journey has been long and intense. Today his challenge has morphed into "being present and being at peace."

ONE PLUS ONE PLUS ONE EQUALS TEN

"It is your role, as Gandhi explained, to share that knowledge with other people."

"I would tell those who are embarking on a new vision, those who are about to create an organization to make the world better, to go for it, absolutely. But don't expect it to be rosy. Don't be naive. If you look at the writings of Mother Theresa, Martin Luther King and Gandhi, the truly heavy weight people, they went through the dark nights of the soul as well. I think it brings you there, and you find yourself extremely lonely in that place. Nobody can be there with you; and you have to process that information, which I call pain, somehow. You are surprised when it hits you; and when it hits you it can really do damage. And when you are damaged, it may stop your ability to make change."

The question becomes, then, one of finding a balance. Where does one *learn* balance? Dr. Amadei thinks it would be helpful for the elders who have gone through this experience to join together share insights. As he says, "One plus one plus one equals ten".

On the horizon is reason for hope. Bernard Amadei is certain that the current generation has begun actively questioning and changing the state of the world. After teaching for more than thirty years, he sees the difference in mindsets. Youth today have lived an entire life with war and with climate change. They are traveling to many countries where they can see for themselves what is actually happening across the world. They care deeply, and they are working to create change. He finds hope in his students, in other youth, and among his colleagues and mentors.

"The allegory of the desert and the oasis has been very important to me in my life. If you want to change the world, you are going to walk into a lot of deserts—deserts of the soul. And you are also going to find a pretty great oasis, and you'll meet some very interesting people along the way. And it is your role, as Gandhi explained, to share that knowledge with other people."

"So bringing the spiritual component, the holistic component, into the discussion is very critical, because short of that, you will be walking in the desert for a long, long time and you will miss the oasis. I walk into the desert only because I know there are some oases, and at those oases I will meet interesting people who have done great work I can learn from. I can teach them some things as well. So it's a place of refreshment, of rest, of camaraderie, and a place that helps you spring forward into the unknown. So that to me is very strong in my life. It's that balance between the desert and the oasis."

RABINDRA MISHRA
Founder, Help Nepal Network

RESTORING THE SOUL OF NEPAL

*"Lots of people were cynical at the beginning about how the
money would be spent. I told them, if we fail, you will lose a dollar.
But if we don't try, we will lose our whole nation."*

Rabindra Mishra couldn't understand why so many poor people in his home country of Nepal were hungry and suffering, some of them starving to death. Nor could he understand why Nepalis who had found success in other countries were doing nothing to sustain their own people.

"I had to ask, where was their generosity? Those individuals who had received foreign educations and made good incomes were staying abroad and ignoring the plight of their own people."

It went against everything Rabindra Mishra learned as a child. His people had always been intrinsically connected to one another—could they no longer feel that? Had they forgotten it was their very interdependence that kept Nepal strong for millennia? Did they no longer remember the ancient Hindu proverb their grandparents had lived by: "May you have enough to eat and give away?"

And then it came to him—he would need to find a way to rekindle the ancient tradition at the heart of the Nepali people's survival, a tradition reflected in their common counsel, "Take a bit of what you have, and share it with your neighbor in need."

This is how the ancient tradition translated into action. At mealtime, every family separated a bit of rice and other food from their cooking pots. They set the food aside, and later delivered it to a needy person or family in their community. Because the practice was followed in nearly every home throughout the land, it sustained each person in multiple ways, including social needs and emotional attachment. No one was ostracized or made to feel inferior, and the poorest among them were equally valued contributors to the community.

From Rabindra's perspective, this tradition ceased to exist sometime between his grandparents' lives and his own generation. To have any hope of restoring the practice, Rabindra knew he would need to dress it in modern ways to fit the evolving Nepali culture. But he also knew he would have to change his own life dramatically; he would have to give up his successful journalism career with the BBC, as well as his comfortable life in London, and devote the rest of his life to restoring the soul of his nation.

Compared to the 11,000 years his ancestors had lived in the region, Rabindra believed that two generations was not so long a time, and that the flame of generosity and cohesiveness could still be revived. Like blowing air on dying embers, he believed that with effort, the spark of compassion could reignite.

Three quarters of the country of Nepal, including its entire northern border with Tibet, lies tucked beneath the towering Himalayan Mountains. The range includes Mount Everest and seven more of the world's tallest peaks, as well as 250 others whose summits jut above 20,000 feet, attracting climbers and trekkers worldwide. If not for these awe-inspiring mountains, you may not have heard much of anything about this land, or the 31 million primarily Hindu people who live in one of the least developed nations in the world.

As it was, few people knew anything about Nepal for centuries. While much of the world developed and grew increasingly interconnected, Nepal's government intentionally isolated its citizens from the outside world. This sequestering, combined with its formidable terrain, made the country inaccessible. As a result, the Nepali people relied solely on the interwoven fabric of their own communities for survival. Though desperately poor, the people of Nepal sustained a strong and vibrant society where individuals relied upon and cared for one another in every possible way.

All of that began to change in 1950 when a palace revolt restored Nepal's ancient monarchy and the new king flung open the country's borders to welcome a modern, yet unknown world. That opening was a turning point that brought seismic changes to a people accustomed to the jolt of devastating earthquakes, but not to the shock of a contemporary world. Seemingly overnight, mountain climbers, journalists, foreign government officials, individuals seeking business opportunities, and a multitude of others surged in from across the world. They brought new customs, new technologies, and a new story of how other people live.

Nepalis relax at the peak of one of its highest mountains.

A period of great flux began. All the wonders of the modern world—previously unknown to Nepal's citizens—were suddenly discovered and desired. Youth began to seek opportunities that would help them afford a more prosperous life, and it wasn't long before they discovered they would need an education to take advantage of all the world was offering. Before Nepal could build adequate colleges or universities, its youth began fleeing to nearby countries to earn degrees. Once educated in academic and worldly ways, few chose to return to what they now considered a backwards and underdeveloped country with little to offer them. Nepal's cohesive society began to unravel.

A GROWING AWARENESS OF THE WORLD

"I was in college when I first began to actively notice beggars in my town. I used to give them some of my pocket change."

Rabindra Mishra grew up in Nepal two decades after that time of great change began, when remnants of his culture's honored traditions gave way to the inevitable changes brought on by foreign visitors and exposure to the modern world. The timing of his birth left him aware of and connected to his country's past, keenly aware of its present challenges, and increasingly concerned for its future.

Like most Nepalis at that time, Rabindra lived in a tiny, remote village far from Kathmandu, the only sizable city in the land. He attended the local school—a fragile hut with few resources. Still, he was a curious and conscientious student, a combination that made him one of the extraordinarily unique students to pass the high school graduation exam.

"In the school I attended, it was rare for even one person to pass the certificate exam required to graduate from high school. In my village, I was that one person. It was so unusual in fact, that I was held up as a hero and carried high around the marketplace, adorned with garland, and vermillion. It was truly a huge celebration for the entire village."

Rabindra left his village to attend the county's first college, located in the city of Kathmandu. His arrival in the country's capital was exhilarating, yet also disconcerting. While village life had not yet felt the changes of modernity, the city had transformed. He witnessed the blight of severe poverty for the first time in his life, and it troubled him deeply.

"I never met my grandparents, so I don't know if my need to help the poor came from their practice. It just started naturally that I felt I needed to do something. I was in college when I first began to actively notice beggars in Kathmandu. I used to give them some of my pocket change."

Seeing those street beggars left Rabindra distraught. The blatant desperation that drove them to the streets simply baffled him. He wondered why city dwellers were not taking care of each other. Why weren't they doing what his parents and grandparents, indeed all of his ancestors, had done to sustain one another going all the way back to ancient and even prehistoric times? Why weren't they separating out a bit of their food at every meal and sharing it with those in need?

After graduating with an English degree, Rabindra was eager to become a journalist. As no graduate schools for journalism had opened in Nepal, he moved 800 miles away to Lahore, Pakistan.

"When I moved to Pakistan I was distressed to see even more poor people there than in Kathmandu. As I traveled on the bus through the city of Lahore, I saw Muslim mothers with four or five children begging on the street. Having grown up in a primarily Hindu country, I wasn't familiar with Islam, and I observed them with great curiosity. When the bus stopped along the route, I was surprised to see people who also appeared to be very poor giving one or two rupees to those begging. This compelling image wouldn't leave my mind. I would later come to learn that for Muslims, giving to others more needy than yourself is a practice known as Zakāt, one of the five pillars of Islam."

After earning a master's degree in Pakistan, Rabindra secured a prize job as a journalist for the BBC in London. Coming from Nepal, the opportunity was a dream. He and his wife settled in London and began having children, and it wasn't long before they began raising them with all the trappings of a prosperous, western life.

THE AWAKENING

"Where was the generosity of successful Nepalis, especially those who had fled to other countries?"

In London, Rabindra began to understand for the first time that money being donated to the poor in Nepal came from individuals living in Western countries. Never realizing this before, it shifted his perception, as he had long believed people in the developed world to be individualistic and disinterested in helping others.

"After seeing how pervasive philanthropy was in London, I came to the conclusion that without these people in the West donating money, there would be no *Action Aid* functioning in Nepal; there would no *Care International* functioning in Nepal; no *Oxfam*, no others if it were true that westerners were only individualistic and not generous. They are generous! It was a shocking revelation."

This awakening expanded as Rabindra followed the news of Charles, Prince of Wales, when he traveled from London to Nepal to visit *Maiti Nepal*, a nonprofit that protects girls victimized by the sex trade from suffering further exploitation. Rabindra followed the story as Prince Charles returned to the UK and immediately created a fund to which he pledged proceeds from his future speeches to help *Maiti Nepal*. Ultimately, he raised 64,000 British pounds, the equivalent of close to $100,000 USD, which he donated in its entirety.

The prince's large donation to help girls in Nepal had a profound impact on Rabindra. He reflected on the three times he had witnessed extreme generosity and benevolence that surprised and inspired him: the poor women in Pakistan who gave rupees to even poorer people; the individuals in London and elsewhere in the West who gave to organizations that helped the poor in Nepal; and finally, Prince Charles, who raised money to help girls in Nepal. While appreciative and humbled by the goodness of strangers who supported the poor and victimized in his country, the largesse began to weigh heavily on him, causing him to face a new and troubling question.

"Where was the generosity of successful Nepalis, especially those who had fled to other countries?"

Those individuals who had received a foreign education and made good incomes were staying abroad and ignoring the plight of their own people. He questioned why strangers were doing for Nepal what they themselves would not. Had Nepalis simply given up and abandoned their homeland? Had he?

"Slowly, I began to feel that is was not enough to be a journalist. I felt it was not enough just to talk about poverty, about service, ideals, and how to change the world. It wasn't enough."

PRACTICAL PHILANTHROPY

Rabindra never met his grandparents, his great grandparents, or his great, great grandparents, and yet they provided the exact inspiration he needed to turn his country around.

Had Rabindra not left Nepal to study, and had he not ultimately found himself living a comfortable life with his wife and children in London, enjoying first rate schools, excellent health care, abundant cultural activities, and a prestigious job at the BBC, he would not have seen and felt the stark contrast when he returned to visit his family and friends in Nepal. He would not have remembered the impact of the first time he saw poor people begging in Kathmandu and Lahore when he was a young man. He would not have noticed how dramatically those scenes contrasted with the experiences and lessons of his youth.

In the end, it was not only abject poverty and starving Nepalis that beckoned him home, it was a horrific and extensive laundry list of problems: blatant and pervasive corruption, substandard health care, antiquated education, an unstable government, choking pollution, a lack of community, and an utter and complete absence of national pride.

It became increasingly obvious to Rabindra that the root cause of the maladies began when Nepal embraced the industrialized world, an event that instigated the loss of the infrangible human connection between them. While it was clear they couldn't and shouldn't try to turn back the clock and reverse progress in Nepal, he began to believe that the once deep connection between the Nepali people could be restored.

Rabindra never met his grandparents, his great grandparents, or his great, great grandparents, and yet they provided the exact inspiration he believed he would need to turn his country around. They had practiced the very thing Rabindra desperately wanted to awaken in his fellow Nepalis... *Practical Philanthropy.*

Of course they didn't call it that, nor did they refer to it at all, because in past generations this was simply a way of life. Because their daily greeting—*May you have enough to eat and give away*—was so integral to their lives, they may have issued those words by rote. However, the actions that prayer-like phrase inspired became the threads that, when woven together, sustained society during his grandparents' lives and for centuries before.

PUSHING CULTURE TO COME FULL CIRCLE

"What I always say is that philanthropy is not just about handing out money. It is about making each and every individual more human. It is about making each and every individual more responsible."

After a period of intense contemplation and many discussions with his wife and other Nepalis in London and Nepal, Rabindra conceived of a plan to create a platform of *Practical Philanthropy.* He recognized that few people in the world could live like Mother Teresa or, in the case of Nepal, Anuradha Koirala, believing as he does that those rare individuals are imbued with exceptional, even divine, qualities. What he felt could be expected, however, is that every Nepali person could begin thinking about those individuals who desperately need help, those who are unable to help themselves.

The road ahead for Rabindra was vague, and felt overwhelming. How does one begin to change a country's mindset and revive their forgotten culture? He and his wife decided if they were going to return to Nepal to take on this challenge, they would need to do so before their eldest child turned ten. After that, it would be difficult for their children to make the adjustment to a developing country, especially one of the poorest and least developed countries in the world.

"It is hard and unusual to move from a first world country to a third world country. Many people derided us for doing so. They thought us cruel to remove our children from a land of opportunity, where education was world class, health care was superior, and life in general was easy. My wife and I felt differently. We knew we could help Nepal, and in fact, we felt we had a responsibility to do so. We also thought our children would truly benefit from the experience. We wanted to teach our children values. What

I always say is that philanthropy is not just about handing out money. It is about making each and every individual more human. It is about making each and every individual more responsible."

He began by quitting his job in London – not easy when you do what you love, are known and respected, and you are well paid. However, he knew it was necessary. When he told his boss at the BBC he was leaving and moving back to Nepal, he responded by offering him an even better position in Nepal. The offer came as a welcome surprise, making him feel as if his decision was the right one. Soon after, they said good-bye to London and began a new life in Kathmandu.

CREATING HELP NEPAL NETWORK: ONE DOLLAR A MONTH FUND FOR NEPAL

"We only asked for $1 a month! Yet even when we asked for $1, we would get 20 questions. People were not used to it in Nepal."

"I began to think of the Nepali people around the world, in the UK, the US, and elsewhere, who, when they visit with each other, tend to talk about Nepal, about politics specifically, because the government is so unstable. There is so much corruption that people don't respect the leaders. This is what they always talk about no matter how long they have been away— what has gone wrong in the country. They say they can't go back and live in Nepal again because of all this corruption, poverty, and so on. But if someone asked them, *'If you feel so passionately about the country's problems, so passionately about the poverty and corruption there, as a Nepali person have you done anything to correct these problems?'* I would say all Nepalis living abroad care deeply about Nepal, and yet most of them would have no answer. They come back to visit every year, and hardly do anything."

Rabindra began by founding the charity Help Nepal Network in 1999, built on the following premise: "Donate whatever you can. Just separate a little bit from what you earn. If you earn a little bit, separate a little bit. If you earn a bit more, separate a bit more, and so on, just as we used to do with food. This is practical philanthropy, and while it won't impact your daily life very much at all, it will help other people immensely. Then perhaps our society can become more egalitarian—not financially egalitarian—*conceptually* egalitarian. As the English say, 'You can't have an island of prosperity in a sea of poverty.'"

He focused his fundraising efforts on Nepalis living around the world and on the wealthy within Nepal. He told them the money raised by the Help Nepal Network, *or HENN*, would go to building schools, health centers, libraries, children's homes, and other life-sustaining infrastructure that the government simply wouldn't or couldn't do. They would also contribute to disaster relief.

They began by asking those who love Nepal around the world to donate at least one dollar a month to the Help Nepal Network.

"We only asked for $1 a month! Yet even when we asked for $1, we would get 20 questions. People were not used to it in Nepal. They thought everything and everybody was corrupt because they were not used to thinking that there are any good people left in Nepal. They thought all the good people moved away, and that nothing good ever happens in Nepal.

"We explained to those living outside that it is the educated people in the country, not the poor people in the villages, who are to be blamed for the corruption and the negative things happening in the country. Poor Nepalis are much more honest, and they are helping build the schools, and the health outposts, and the libraries. They are good people, honest, and hard working. We continued to prove that good things were happening with funds that were being donated, and slowly our support base increased.

"They were asking exactly how the money would be used. We told them we would not spend one penny on anything but the work itself. From the beginning, we separated the administrative arm from the charitable arm. This is very different than most non-profits and charities that normally they take 10-20% of their donations to fund the administration. We used our own money and we all worked as volunteers."

As the donations began to grow, and they began constructing schools and medical outposts throughout the country, Rabindra could see they needed a small coordinating office in Kathmandu.

Villagers wait in line to visit a health worker at a HENN-funded clinic.

"Initially that was difficult to fund. So I searched to find 25 Nepalis who were willing to give $4,000 each to set up the Help Nepal Administrative Endowment fund of $100,000. It was difficult. I wrote and spoke with many, many individuals and eventually I was able to raise it. You can find the names of these people on the Help Nepal website, in addition to my wife and myself, who each gave $4,000.

"We were really persistent, and we proved that good things could happen in Nepal. And we showed them that there are good people left.

"Lots of people were cynical at the beginning about how the money would be spent. I told them, if we fail, you will lose a dollar. But if we don't try, we will lose our whole nation. We told them, 'We are young people trying to build something. If we misuse the money, we will lose our reputation, our image, and we'll lose our future. And we are ready to take that risk.'"

By Western standards, a dollar a month can sound negligible – perhaps not worth bothering over. In Nepal, it's a small fortune.

"You can't imagine what one dollar can do in Nepal. One dollar makes a huge difference, a *huge* difference! There is one mother here who recently committed suicide with her daughter, because she couldn't feed her. In the last hour, 1,000 people have died from hunger or hunger-related problems in the world. In Nepal, in the last hour, four children have died because they lack the most basic medical facility."

This deplorable and unnecessary situation frustrates Rabindra deeply, and as he discusses it his voice reveals a mixture of anger and deep sadness.

"In a society like Nepal, we became so self-centered that we stopped thinking about posterity, we stopped thinking about the future, and we just wanted to do things for ourselves. For example, it doesn't make sense for a rich person to spend $25,000 for a bottle of wine when children are dying in Asia and Africa. And yet, they do."

With greater trust came more donations and *HENN* began constructing more health outposts, building and expanding schools, and opening libraries in rural areas. Eventually they started to fill them with computers and books. Slowly, some Nepalis began to believe progress could actually be made. They began to believe what few had thought possible—that the cohesiveness of the Nepali culture and community may finally be returning.

THE COLOSSAL CHALLENGES OF RAISING MONEY IN NEPAL

"Please, go back to your poor village where you grew up and help just one child to get an education."

Anyone charged with raising money for charity in a developed country understands the enormous challenges one faces. When an organization is new and unknown, it's a steep and difficult road.

That's the case even in countries where tax laws are designed to support the non-profit sector. Those laws help create a culture of philanthropy, promoting the philosophy that society should take care of it's own. In addition to government support, charities in such countries also rely on faith institutions, the media, the entertainment industry, and even peer pressure to encourage individuals and companies to donate money.

In Nepal, the exact opposite mindset prevails. No tax deductions are allowed for charitable giving. That means all motivation must come from the heart, not financial incentives. Even those who did wish to donate money readily assumed corruption, meaning Rabindra needed to change the popular belief from *Those who give money to charities are naïve,* to *Those who give money can save our country.*

HENN provides healthy meals to young students in a Nepali village.

Of the 3 million Nepalis who live outside its borders, 1.5 million work in the Gulf region, and are very poor. They sold their properties and traveled there to make money to support their children. Another 1.5 million Nepalis live in the West, and have relatively nice lives. These richer expatriates are the primary focus of his campaign. He pushes them to go beyond the $1 a month campaign if they can.

"I ask them, 'Please, go back to your poor village where you grew up, and help just one child to get an education.' If they did, 1.5 million children would get good educations, and this would help the country tremendously. These Nepali people abroad have seen quite clearly what poverty is. Most of them have experienced poverty in their own family. Somehow they, like myself, were fortunate."

Rabindra has no trouble asking his fellow citizens to donate. "If you are fully confident, you can ask them to do this. If people don't want to help with their own village and they have the money, it is probably them who should feel uncomfortable saying no, not me feeling uncomfortable asking them."

Asking Nepali expats to donate to their home country succeeded far beyond Rabindra's expectations. Though it has taken several years to build, the network now has chapters in fourteen countries, including Australia, Austria, Canada, Denmark, Ireland, Nepal, New Zealand, Qatar, Russia, Saudi Arabia, South Korea, Sweden, United Kingdom, and the United States.

Nepali expatriates living in Finland gather in support of Help Nepal Network.

Having seen the concept of corporate responsibility taking root in Western nations, Rabindra thought it would be wise to see if Nepali businesses were on the same path. His efforts were met with disappointment. He cites corporate responsibility in Nepal as being almost completely ineffective, because without a sense of personal responsibility among corporate employees, there can be no such thing as 'corporate social responsibility.' Regardless of how many zero's you add together, the total remains zero.

"I tell these bankers that when people without a sense of personal responsibility sit around a nice table and talk about the importance of corporate social responsibility, it simply doesn't work because the individuals personally don't have that feeling. When they try to do or change something as an institution, it is only a gesture. It doesn't actually change anything. It makes people feel like they tried to change something, and then they are free."

Rather than waiting on corporate Nepal or any entity to develop a sense of giving, he found yet another to way to speed up progress.

PHILANTHROPIC JOURNALISM – ANOTHER ARROW IN THE QUIVER

"I was invited onto TV and radio shows to give analysis about politics, I hobnobbed with famous people… and yet, I really hadn't done anything to make tangible change."

When Rabindra attempted to resign from the BBC to return to Nepal and was instead offered the position as Editor of Nepal Service, he was elated to continue working in the field of journalism. There was more to it than providing an income. He began to see a way he could directly boost his goal to reconnect Nepali people to each other using journalism.

As Editor of the Nepali service, he manages the team, guides editorial aspects, and also continues to work as a journalist. In other words, he was perfectly positioned to reach the people of Nepal with an entirely new approach.

The BBC World Service has 27 language services around the world, and Nepali is one of the smallest. And yet, as Rabindra describes it, "The BBC has a huge impact in Nepal. We have 6 million regular listeners.

"As I worked with BBC and other media, I came to the conclusion that the field of journalism had not been as active in public service as it could be, neither in Nepal nor anywhere around the world. Journalism is entirely focused on bad news; that is how we are groomed. From the morning, if you listen to CNN, BBC, Al Jazeera, The Guardian, Time Magazine, and so on, you see that journalism is all about conflict, disaster, political wrangling, regime change... all negative events. That is the dominant feature of journalism. And you ask yourself, has this changed the world for the better? Has it actually served the public, which is the core value of journalism? My conclusion was, 'No, it had not.'"

Other journalists may counter that argument by listing the many ways they have helped promote democracy by holding authorities accountable, by exposing corruption, and by exposing all the negatives happening in society. However, Rabindra argues that by focusing on bad news 24 hours a day, journalism is creating negative vibes rather than positive vibes.

"Just as political battles, disasters, and killings are happening around the world, there are many good things happening as well. There are many good people doing good things."

So, in concert with the work he does through Help Nepal, Rabindra set out to change the fundamental understanding of what journalism is. Given the enormous strength, power, and access that journalism holds, it can be a serious catalyst for change.

He's not the first to broach the issue. In the 1970's, academics came up with the idea of *developmental journalism*. The idea was to bring attention to actual issues of development. That was a step forward. But others believed that that wasn't enough. So in the 1990's, another group of journalists came up with the idea of *public journalism*. The idea was to encourage journalists to share ideas of their concern. To some extent, this promoted debate on issues among the public, inviting discussion from the public. This was also progress.

However, as Rabindra saw it, the problem with both of these approaches was that they were bringing up new topics of discussion with the hope that some authority or brilliant philanthropist would take action. The journalist thought they had done their duty, but he sees it differently.

"We shouldn't leave journalism at that point. Let's say we take a photo of children who are forced to take classes outside under a tree because they have no classroom, which happens regularly. A journalist shows this photo, adding a couple lines that say: 'If anyone is interested in helping build a school, they can contact the following', and provide the name of the principal and give the school number. 'The cost would be $5,000.'"

Nepali students jostle to get a peek inside their new school.

"Then someone may come forward and help that school. So my proposition is, don't just raise the issue; show the way that the issue can be addressed. I call that action *philanthropic journalism*. Listen, if you can have sports journalism, if you can have political journalism, if you can environmental journalism, if you can have economic journalism, if you can have entertainment journalism, why can't you have philanthropic journalism, whereby you actually try to resolve the real issues?"

So he took another bold step. He stopped writing his extremely popular political column and started writing a column focused solely on philanthropic journalism.

"I thought, okay, I write a political analysis and get a call from a politician telling me how great it was, as well as messages on Facebook and email saying it was a brilliant analysis. I realized that all the praise does not trigger things. It makes one feel good; makes one feel he is doing brilliantly. For me, it gave me public fame. I was invited onto TV and radio shows to give analysis about politics, I hobnobbed with famous people... and yet, I hadn't really done anything using journalism to make tangible change."

Surprisingly to Rabindra and others, people loved his new column. They told him they were so tired and fed up with the day in day out side of politics. They found it very refreshing to read about how individuals were doing small things to help one another.

"Sometimes my articles show up on the front page. People began talking about philanthropy and charity. I began seeing a buzz. A change."

TANGIBLE CHANGES AND VALUES CHANGE

"I am not a rich person, I am a middle class person, and whatever I have earned, the relatively comfortable life I am living—nothing gives me satisfaction like these two things I am doing with Help Nepal Network and philanthropic journalism."

In April 25, 2015, a massive earthquake struck Nepal, followed by hundreds of aftershocks in the following days and weeks. All told, more than 8500 people lost their lives and 23,000 were injured. By that time the Help Nepal Network was well developed and trusted—a significant accomplishment in itself. As a result, Help Nepal was able to raise more than 1 million USD to help the survivors. The money was used to mobilize teams of volunteers to reach areas that most charities couldn't get to, and to provide tents, food, and medical supplies for the thousands of displaced.

To date, Help Nepal has built or expanded more than 40 schools in villages across the country. They have established more than 40 libraries, constructed a large home for orphaned children, purchased thousands of computers and supplies for schools and libraries, opened blood transfusion centers, built multiple health centers, provided wheel chairs, stretchers and other medical supplies, sponsored dental, vision and hearing camps, rescued and aided hundreds of thousands of earthquake survivors, and much, much more.

"The world has developed so much. We have made incredible strides in technology, in academics, in science, in economics. But throughout the world, gaps between the rich and poor are increasing, environmental degradation is increasing, the sense of insecurity is increasing, and violence is increasing. So our generation, with all of our knowledge, and all of our economic achievements, must address this problem. Unless and until each and every individual who is able to look after himself or herself starts to think about somebody else, the world won't change."

Starting Help Nepal has impacted Rabindra in a very positive way. It gives him a sense of profound satisfaction and a deep sense of happiness, which his chosen profession alone could not provide.

"I try to practice and promote values that I uphold in my life. I am not a rich person, I am a middle class person, and whatever I have earned, the relatively comfortable life I am living—nothing gives me satisfaction like these two things I am doing with Help Nepal Network and philanthropic journalism. So yes, this work has changed me—it has changed my kids. And they see what I am accomplishing in Nepal, and that impacts them positively."

For a person to succeed in making change, especially the scale of change Rabindra and his colleagues have accomplished, he believes three things are necessary.

"First, find peace with your inherent greed. It so easy to appreciate the value of doing so—but so difficult to follow. It is easy to praise good people, but it is difficult to be good yourself.

"Second, one has to believe that in order for a person to be happy, the people around us have to be happy as well. One has to believe in that; one cannot be happy in isolation.

"Third, persevere. Many people want to change things, but they lose their perseverance when it gets tough, and they start to make excuses. Because it can, and does, get tough. I hear people say they wanted to do things, they tried, but people didn't listen and didn't care about it. It was so difficult. They had to go to the government offices, they couldn't get what they needed...all kinds of excuses. But that is precisely why you have to do it. If there weren't challenges the problem wouldn't be there for you to fix. It is difficult and it's why people often let obstacles take over. But you have to tear those obstacles apart."

Rabindra believes every individual who has enough ability and resources to look after his or her own family can do a great deal to change their own society and the world.

"The examples we give to our children are that they have to own things, they have to be rich, they have to be famous. Not many teach that you have be successful, but you have to be a good human being as well. One hardly hears this, so most people are running after fame and fortune until their last breath.

"I will continue to do what I am doing as I am happy and fortunate, especially compared to the hundreds of thousands of people in Nepal who find it difficult to simply survive. There is nothing for me to complain about. I am at peace in my life."

As for the people of Nepal, while they continue to face new hardships brought on by the devastating earthquakes last year, along with entrenched poverty, corruption, and many of the problems they had when Help Nepal started over fifteen years ago, there are significant differences. Hundreds of orphans now have a safe place to call home. Thousands more students attend schools in actual buildings. Tens of thousands more Nepalis have access to medical care. Educational achievements are growing. Untold numbers have been rescued, fed, housed, and cared for after their villages were destroyed by earthquakes.

The most significant change is not measured by statistics, nor will it ever be. Rather, it shows up in the smile of strangers when they meet on the street. It is revealed in the gratefulness of a widow kept alive by her neighbor's generosity. It is found in the joy of a donor who writes a check to a charity, confident the money will reach it's intended destination. It shows up as renewed pride in the voice of a Nepali expat living overseas, as he or she states proudly, "Yes, I come from Nepal".

The arrival of new computers changes everything for these eager students.

Closer to home, it shows up in the eyes of Rabindra's children, grateful to be living in the home of their ancestors, eager to be part of Nepal's rebirth, proud to be the children of a man who wouldn't accept the demise of his country, but who continues to give his heart and soul to restore it to glory.

CHRISTOPHER CATRAMBONE
Founder, Migrant Offshore Aid Station

SAVING LIVES AT SEA:
THE WORLD'S MOST DANGEROUS BORDER CROSSING

*"The people getting on these smuggler boats are well aware they might die.
But their lives are so bad that it's worth the risk to them. They tell us,
'It's Europe or die'. It's that clear for them. I have had poets on board,
scholars—beautiful people you would imagine sitting
and talking with in a café."*

Christopher Catrambone saves the lives of hopeful migrants who would otherwise drown at sea. It's that straightforward. For the nearly 15,000 individuals he and his team have rescued from the Mediterranean, Aegean, and Andaman Seas in the past two years, it's all that matters.

The saga of how and why he came to do this work is an interwoven story of conscious and subconscious beliefs, life-altering experiences, and deeply held values that fused together, define the man. Whether he's living out his main vocation, or volunteering his time and money as he is when rescuing migrants, his life has always been centered on helping innocent people in harm's way.

Christopher and his wife Regina founded the Migrant Offshore Aid Station, or *MOAS* in 2014 after purchasing and refitting the *M.Y. Phoenix*—a solidly-built, albeit decaying, 130-foot expedition vessel. After hauling the un-seaworthy vessel from the eastern coast of the United States to their home on the island of Malta, it took several more months and millions of dollars to make the boat suitable for what would truly become sacred work.

The story really began years earlier in the city of New Orleans, where Christopher was a graduate student in Sociology and Criminology at Loyola University. On the pivotal day of August 28, 2005, he was fortunate to be 850 miles away conducting research in Nassau, Bahamas. Fortunate, because that's the day Hurricane Katrina, one of the most violent storms in U.S. history, slammed into New Orleans, overwhelming the levee system and submerging 80% of the city under water. Katrina took the lives of more than 1800 people, and ruined the lives of thousands more.

Though eager to return to the home and life he loved in New Orleans, as well as to complete his degree, Christopher soon learned there was quite literally no way to do that. So much of the city was destroyed that it would be years before life there returned to normal.

Making the best of a bad situation, Christopher chose to wait out the recovery period on the island of St. Thomas where he had ample work to do. Always the ambitious entrepreneur, he had already begun building an international claims-assistance business while in college, and with two employees on his staff, he knew he could spend the time expanding his business until it was possible for him to return home.

Meanwhile, he convinced two good friends to join him in St. Thomas until the situation improved. Both men were accomplished New Orleans chefs who lost their jobs when Katrina destroyed the restaurants where they worked. The three friends pooled the hurricane relief funds they had each received from the government and opened an authentic, New Orleans-style restaurant named *Cajun Mary's* on an old Riverboat on St. Thomas Island.

"Cajun Mary's was our psychological help. We recreated our New Orleans culture, and people started coming from nearby islands to eat authentic, Creole food."

Though the restaurant was hugely successful, when the chefs' respective restaurants reopened one year later, they closed Cajun Mary's and the two moved back to New Orleans.

For Christopher, things were different. He soon discovered, as refugees often do, that he could never go home again. Upon entering his house in New Orleans, he found it looted and in ruins. Literally everything was gone—a lifetime of photographs and all his personal belongings. In many ways it felt as if his past life had been vanquished. Most difficult, however, was the discovery that nearly everyone he knew had fled the city with no plans to return.

"New Orleans was still so raw, even after a year. One of the real back-stories of the creation of *MOAS* was my personal understanding of someone seeking refuge after having to flee their home. I didn't have a place to go back to after Katrina. Luckily, I had created a job that wasn't centralized in New Orleans; it was only based there."

Christopher decided he would need to start over somewhere else, yet had no idea where to go. It was a difficult, gut-wrenching time. He felt unattached, and had a deep need to set down roots and find connection somewhere.

"After a great deal of thought, I picked up and moved to Reggio, Italy."

NEW LIFE IN THE OLD WORLD

"I have to admit it has been dangerous work. I've almost been killed many times, in Afghanistan for one. The closest I came to death was in the north of Israel in 2008 or 2009, when a Katyusha rocket hit the house next door and blew it up."

Reggio is located in the Calabria region in southern Italy, a beautiful town set in the toe of the Italian boot. When he arrived, Christopher happily discovered that his family name, Catrambone—one Americans had rarely pronounced properly—was immediately recognized and correctly articulated. That wasn't a total surprise, as his great-grandparents had emigrated to the United States from Sicily in the 1800's. Still, it made him feel welcomed and at home.

"If you can go anywhere in the world to start over, why not go to the place where you can explore your roots, your genealogy?"

So he settled in, and it wasn't long before Christopher began further expanding his insurance claims company into the successful and highly respected *Tangiers Group.*

While living in Calabria, Christopher fell in love with Regina, a beautiful local woman who had a young daughter named Maria Luisa. They married soon after, and at the age of 23, Christopher became father to a nine-year-old girl. He moved his new family to picturesque Malta, an archipelago of islands located in the Mediterranean Sea fifty miles south of Sicily. Malta is a former British colony that won its independence in 1964, so the population there is English speaking. Most of Tangiers's clients spoke English as well, so Christopher felt comfortable running his business from there.

Looking back at his life now, it is easy to see how the pieces, physical and emotional, were leading him toward a mission to help North African and Middle Eastern migrants find safe passage to Italy. Yet at the time, there was no way to foresee the twists ahead, and there was more work to be done that would prepare him for the enormous challenges he would face.

As his insurance business continued to expand, he found opportunity in a new market, providing coverage to individuals working in high-risk situations in countries that no insurance companies wanted to touch. Which is how, in 2008, Christopher's business took a turn to Iraq where he began setting up medical facilities to serve Iraqis, Africans, Fijians, and others who were injured while working for foreign companies in the war-torn country. These workers had nowhere to seek treatment for their injuries, and those who weren't from Iraq had no way to get transported back to their home countries to recuperate. Many had serious injuries, such as multiple amputations, and were essentially stranded in Iraq with little or no medical assistance.

"There was a real cry for help in Iraq. And all it really required was someone to set up the coordination and logistics. I showed up one day, and just started talking to hospital administrators. Then I hired a few doctors. It was a bit nerve-wracking, as there is no military protecting you. No security following you around. You are just a normal person there to do business. But you are doing it for the purpose of helping people.

"To this day, we are still operating in Iraq and still running this program. We saved thousands of people, and then we did the same thing in Afghanistan, on a bigger scale. I used the same model there, and now have replicated it in over sixty of the hardest countries in the world to assist people medically and to evacuate those in need. No one else is really doing this because it takes actually going into these countries, which are often war zones, and building relationships with the people living there. All of these programs are still thriving today. They aren't all networks. In some countries we own hospitals and clinics, with our own doctors overseeing the work of local doctors.

"We want to be sure that people are getting the very best possible medical treatment available because they each deserve as good or better care than anyone in the US or in other western countries get. They don't deserve to get inferior health care in a battlefield hospital when they are getting their leg amputated. It's ridiculous."

It becomes clearer with every story that Christopher is a rescuer at heart, and he cares deeply about people. Though he has made a profit doing it, often it has come at great risk to himself.

"I have to admit it has been dangerous work. I've almost been killed many times, in Afghanistan for one. The closest I came to death was in the north of Israel in 2008 or 2009, when a Katyusha rocket hit the house next door and blew it up. I have had about 50 cases where I have to find a person who we insured, and make sure they are okay. This particular time I was warned not to go down into this area where he was, but I had to see if he was okay. So I found him in his bunker, and as I was leaving a rocket struck the house next door and completely blew it up. I was okay, but of all my travels across Africa, Asia and the Middle East, that was the closest call I had.

"You cannot be afraid of death. I'm not overly religious, but I keep a nice prayer—a psalm, actually—with me when I go to these places. My faith in God really does keep me. If it's my time, it's my time. Not that I act crazy and go jump into a bomb-infested area. I'm going to use my brain. But at the same time, I have faith that when I'm out there God will protect me. My family and I are Catholic; my brother-in-law is a priest in Italy. So we are people of faith, yet we believe in all religions. We believe that just because we are Catholic doesn't mean ours is the right one; I believe everybody's religion is right. I think all religions are very similar in that they try to teach us stories about how to live our lives.

"Since I married Regina, and began raising our daughter, I became more careful. They became my reason to come back home after I traveled. It was then I began to limit my trips to the world's hotspots, because I didn't want to leave my family. Today I no longer travel to Iraq and Afghanistan."

The Tangiers Group would become financially successful in a span of just a few years. They added intelligence and ground information for people traveling into dangerous regions, with many of their products backed by the infamous Lloyds of London. Christopher also expanded into insurance brokerage, and today Tangiers covers all Air Malta planes, non-combat drones, and more.

YACHTING IN THE MEDITERRANEAN

"So here I am, on a luxury cruise with my wife and daughter, celebrating everything we had accomplished. And while we are on the water, we face the reality that people are drowning in those same waters on the hopes of getting to where we are. Why are we allowing them to die?"

As hard working as Christopher clearly is, he was in need of a serious vacation. In 2013, he decided a break was in order. He loved spending time with his wife and daughter, and thus chartered a beautiful yacht where they could spend three glorious weeks sailing around the Mediterranean Sea.

"I loved doing that, because there are no distractions, no phones. It is just so pure being out there that way."

With a professional captain and crew, and a highly-rated chef, everything was in place for a stretch of deep relaxation. One afternoon, after finishing a delicious lunch of tuna tartare, Christopher and his wife were sitting and relaxing as the yacht sailed along, when Regina spotted a tan jacket floating in the water. As they were far from any coast, she wondered how a coat could end up there, in the middle of the sea. She decided to ask the captain about it. The answer she received was sobering.

"The coat most likely belonged to one of the migrants who drowned fleeing North Africa for Italy. There are thousands who drown each year trying to escape the particular hell they are living in."

Regina and Christopher looked at one another, taken aback. It was a poignant moment for them both. Later, they docked at Maritime, a small island off the Sicilian coast. After dinner they began discussing the deplorable migrant situation with the yacht's captain, Marco Cauchi. As a 20-year veteran of Malta's Armed Services and Commander of a Patrol Vessel, Marco had rescued untold numbers of migrants in the Mediterranean, and understood their plight.

"You have to understand," Christopher explains with emotion, "Marco is a hero in every possible way. He has saved so many lives at sea. On that trip, he told Regina and I one story that continues to haunt Marco to this day, involving a migrant from Eritrea. She was a young, pregnant woman he rescued while he was commander of a Malta Navy vessel. They had rescued a boatful of people, and moved them safely onto the Navy vessel. She was rescued, and she was safe. But then she fell off the ship back into the ocean. It became clear she couldn't swim and was dropping down like an anchor. Fully clothed, Marco dove straight into the water to try and save her. She was sinking fast, and Marco kept swimming deeper and deeper to catch her. His arms were outreached to her and hers were reaching for his, but he just couldn't get to her. Finally, he had swum so deep he physically couldn't go any further. He told us that every night since that happened, when he closes his eyes, he sees her eyes staring at him in her last moments and her unborn child's last moments."

Marco looked at Christopher and Regina and asked, "How can we be letting this happen? How can people be drowning and we're doing nothing to save them?"

Another day they docked at Rabbit Island, tucked 100 miles off the Italian coast. Rabbit Beach is considered by many to be one of the world's most beautiful beaches in the world. Despite the glorious crystal clear waters and white sandy beaches, their thoughts were back at sea with the migrants, and their time there was punctuated by stories of migrants' bodies washing up on the beach.

"So here I am, on a luxury cruise with my wife and daughter, celebrating everything we had accomplished. And while we are on the water, we face the reality that people are drowning in those same waters on the hopes of getting to where we are. Why are we allowing them to die? It just sounds so ridiculous! If you are a real person, with any feelings, and you think, 'Okay, here I am out here spending a ton of money chartering a vessel, eating shrimp and tuna tartare every day, and at the same time in these same waters, people are trying to escape war, poverty, and abuse to get their civil and human rights.' So they are out there dying and we are out there playing around. It was just a huge wake up call for us! So we said, 'You know what, we've been successful. We've been getting paid to save lives for a long time and we know how. Now is the time for us to give back and save lives with the money we have.'"

POLITICS OVER PEOPLE

"This is the most disgusting thing in the world to allow people to die with so much hope in their hearts. That's what I find to be so crushing."

Christopher is a businessman, not an activist. Yet once he and Regina came to fully understand the situation of migrants drowning at tragic rates, they were not willing to look away or stand by without rescuing as many people as they possibly could. In the weeks following their vacation, they continued to seek more information about the migrant situation.

The majority of migrants are young men, though an increasing number are women, some of whom are pregnant. Some women become impregnated by rape on their journey to their debarkation point in Libya, their bodies bartered by the smugglers to get them past border agents. Other migrants are families with babies and young children in tow. They know the risks, and they know the odds are against them making it to Europe alive, but the hope for a better life is far stronger than the fear that might stop them.

It is a situation that disturbs Christopher endlessly. "I remember being young and having hope that something would work out, with one problem or another, but always having hope. If you put yourself in the place of these women with their children, they just have nothing left but hope that they will reach a land where they can be free. Where they can survive. Where they believe they will have their human rights respected. And then all of that hope is crushed when they drown at sea. This is the most disgusting thing in the world to allow people to die with so much hope in their hearts. That's what I find to be so crushing. I know what its like to be displaced. I know what its like to be poor. I know what it's like to have to leave your home and survive on nothing but hope."

Those willing to risk the perilous journey are everyday people escaping war, violence, persecution, extreme poverty, and other hardships in their home countries. They come from across North Africa, from sub-Saharan Africa, from Syria, Iraq, and elsewhere in the Middle East. African migrants are often held for one to two months in so-called "connection houses" in Libya, now a lawless country on the north shore of Africa with a straight route to Italy.

Those who languish in connection houses with other migrants are repeatedly subjected to violence and abuse by the human smugglers to whom they have paid between $1600 and $5000 US—their entire life savings, for only the sea portion of the trip. Many have had to pay similar amounts for land transport to get to Libya. Most have sold all their possessions to raise money, or acquired money from their family and other villagers, and travel with only the clothes on their back.

Regardless which continent they are fleeing, when they are ready for departure the smugglers pack their human cargo in less-than-seaworthy boats, filling every inch. Once it's full, they add more people—a lot more. The unwieldy, heavy boats are navigated out to sea with insufficient drinking water and no life jackets, save those worn by the rare few who could pay $100 extra. Once the boats clear the coast, the smugglers abandon the doomed rafts or boats, leaving only a compass behind. As they jump into speedboats sent to retrieve them, they point the nearly sinking boats in the direction of Italy. From Libya, it's a rough, 300 miles to the closest Italian island of Lampedusa. Their greatest hope for survival is being rescued by a seaworthy vessel capable of accommodating hundreds of people.

That's where European politics enter the story.

With chaos and violence increasing in many African countries in recent years, as well as the war in Syria moving into it's sixth year, the number of desperate people escaping by sea has skyrocketed. Many do not survive the journey. Some migrants die from the cold and hypothermia, while others on the same boat survive. In some cases, entire boats capsize with all or nearly all on board drowning. Other times there are shipwrecks like the one that occurred off the Italian island of Lampedusa in October of 2013, which took the lives of nearly 400 trapped migrants. The absolute horror of that tragedy—the bodies of one mother and baby were found still attached by the umbilical cord—prompted outrage, and a demand for action.

The Italian government stepped up the following month with money and life-saving resources, launching a search and rescue operation named *Mare Nostrum* that was immediately successful in saving lives. In just one year, *Mare Nostrum* was credited with saving more than 174,000 immigrants from a near certain death at sea. They did more than rescue them, however. They also provided medical treatment, shelter and food. In addition, they helped many with legal assistance to gain asylum either in Italy or elsewhere in Europe.

But money and politics ensured that *Mare Nostrum* was short lived. The Italian government ended the *Mare Nostrum* program in November of 2014, one year after it began, leaving the now surging number of migrants to fend for themselves.

THE LAUNCH OF MOAS - MIGRANT OFFSHORE AID STATION

"Let's not overcomplicate this. People are drowning. Let's pull them out of the water! Who cares about the politics? If you want to take them and place them wherever you want afterward, fine; at least they don't die at sea in Europe's back door."

"One day it came to me clearly. I can sit here in my house, with this beautiful view of the ocean, and I know people are dying out there. And I know I have a skill that no one else has on this island of Malta. I know I can save lives. I know technically how to do it. Once I know all that, then it's on me. So I realized, if I'm ever going to do this, now is the time; when I am 33 years old, not 65 years old. The time is now."

Christopher and Regina had seen the floating coat on their yachting trip, heard many personal stories of migrant deaths from the captain, and heard more stories of bodies washing up on Rabbit Beach. Then they heard the horrific news of the tragic accident that killed nearly 400 migrants on an island just 100 miles away from their home in Malta.

"My wife, Regina, often cites Jesus's words to us that we have to sow seeds. That's what we wanted to do. Save lives and sew seeds. We agree with Pope Francis, who spoke out this year, saying we are battling the *'globalization of indifference'*, as he termed it. And it's true."

So began the work to establish *MOAS*, or Migrant Offshore Aid Station, a non-profit organization with a mission to save as many lives at sea as possible. Christopher hired Marco Cauchi, the captain of their life-changing yachting vacation, to head up search and rescue operations. During his time in the armed services he had been Search Mission Coordinator, rescuing thousands from the sea over a twenty-year period.

Next came the all-important search for someone to direct the organization. They were very fortunate to find the perfect man, Martin Xuereb, a highly educated Maltese native who once headed the Maltese army, and also served as a diplomat in Brussels. Like Marco, he had his own difficult memories of experiences with migrant death that inspired him to join *MOAS*. He tells of an 8-year old Syrian boy who had died at sea. When they unzipped the body bag for the boy to be identified, he was staring right at Martin with eyes wide open. Martin couldn't remove that young face from his mind, nor stop wondering what the last thing he saw was before he died.

"People who experience the passing of those who risked death in the hope of living, or of living a decent life, are inspired to do something. So one of the biggest missions of *MOAS* is to humanize this issue, to show the world that these migrants are real people. We need to let the world know these are human beings dying out there. And we don't have to roll out the red carpet for them, just give them a chance to live."

THE M.Y. PHOENIX RISES

"We are in the 21st century! Can't we find a tool that is more modern and accurate than binoculars?"

Christopher is smitten. "The Phoenix is a beautiful boat—she is also a beast. Built in 1973, her hull is more than 5 meters deep —as deep as a warship's hull. She is the deepest and most expansive expedition vessel of that size in the world. They do not build anything else like her today."

The vessel, which can rescue up to 350 people at a time, needed to be repaired and refitted to serve the needs of the mission. They built a huge flight deck on the back, which can double as a special area for men and women who need to be separated due to their religious beliefs.

The M.Y. Phoenix patrolling the Mediterranean Sea.

"You may have Muslims and Christians on board, and there are huge cultural sensitivities to consider. We want the women and children to have separate and private bathroom facilities. There is a respect for their privacy."

Then came the technology. "When we first started, I said, 'We are in the 21st century! Can't we find a tool that is more modern and accurate than binoculars?' I mean, why not?"

"We decided to use drones, because they are a very crucial tool that allow us to find a boat within 5 minutes, as opposed to 6 hours using binoculars or other mundane tools. Within seconds or minutes, we can find any boat in the area, with the clarity of being able to see exactly what is happening on the boat. The thermal imaging feature allows us to operate around the clock, so we can find boats in the dark."

MOAS would need a way to transport the migrants from their precarious, sinking crafts to the larger Phoenix, so they purchased two, rigid-hulled inflatable boats for the job. The RHIBS, as they are called, can zip across the water to the troubled vessel, rescue those in distress, and bring them in turns to the main vessel.

THE RESCUES BEGIN

"The very first passenger we brought on board was a six-month old baby."

With a captain, crew, equipment, and a refitted vessel, *MOAS* was ready to begin saving lives. They inaugurated the operation on August 25, 2014, setting sail from Malta's Grand Harbor.

It took only five days before they were called to assist 250 stranded Syrians and Palestinians, 40 of them children. The same day they assisted in the rescue of nearly 100 migrants from Sub-Saharan Africa, who needed help moving from a rubber dinghy to a rescue vessel.

It would be less than two weeks out on the sea before they made their first large rescue onto the Phoenix. Once they located the distressed ship using the drones, they jumped into the RHIBS and sped toward the boat.

Jason Florio, a *MOAS* photographer who documented the first rescue, was overwhelmed when he saw the faces on board.

"When I saw the first boat we approached, I could hardly hold back my tears. You are never prepared for such a sight. What is striking is the sudden quietness of the people on the boat, their sense of relief for realizing we are there to save them. Then comes the agitation, as they rush to be rescued first, fearing they are going to be left behind."

A recently rescued young girl rides along with her mother and baby sister on the deck of the Phoenix headed for Italy.

Despite his own emotions, Christopher remained intensely focused on the logistics of the rescue. "Everyone gets a life jacket immediately, before anything else, because we don't know how quickly their boat is going to sink. The second thing we do is hydrate them before we start to move them.

"On that first rescue, I looked closely at every single person we saved as they boarded the RHIBS. In addition to the men, there were 83 women and children in the boat, the youngest, a mere two days old. It was a deeply emotional day for everyone. My wife, Regina, and our 19-year old daughter, Maria Luisa, were engaged in the post-rescue on the *Phoenix*, helping the women and the babies. I had to fight with Regina to take Maria Luisa on, but she really wanted to be there. Everyone was helping.

"The very first passenger we brought on board was a six-month old baby. We had a crib on board, and I remember when they handed me the baby, and I carried him to our onboard doctor. As I passed through the crew I could see all twenty people who had been working for six months to get these rescues started. The crew, mostly men, had these huge eyes, amazed by what was unfolding. I remember the chief officer on board, a man from Poland in his sixties, and when he saw that baby he just had tears running down his cheeks.

"Everybody on board who experienced that was a changed person. They saw what we saw, and they believed in the mission 100%. The people, the children, are so innocent. You know that these little children have absolutely no idea why they are on this boat, or what is going on."

In the first two weeks of operation, *MOAS* would rescue some 1500 migrants. These were staggering numbers for the brand new operation. The next month would bring the rescue of another 1500 migrants before the operation ended for the year, as weather stepped in to make the journey too treacherous for even the smugglers to risk.

Now hydrated and wearing MOAS-provided life jackets,
a very full boat of fleeing migrants eagerly await boarding the Phoenix.

THE PURE NECESSITY OF COLLABORATION

"MOAS is now finding the migrants and rescuing them, and Médecins Sans Frontières is handling the health of the migrants on board."

Anyone who has built a successful organization of any kind appreciates the value and necessity of working with others to achieve the mission. When *Médecins Sans Frontières* (Doctors without Borders) contacted Christopher in the spring of 2015, he jumped at the opportunity to meet with them. It didn't take long to sign an agreement to bring their doctors on board the *Phoenix* to provide post-rescue assistance to the migrants.

Sharing their mission with such a large, well-known organization brought a large cash infusion as well; one million dollars toward the operation of the *Phoenix*. MOAS and MSF are now partners in the business of savings lives at sea.

"So *MOAS* is now finding the migrants and rescuing them, and *MSF* is handling the health of the migrants on board. Last year we employed hundreds of doctors and paramedics, linguists, mental health professionals... it's what we bring in credibility to our project that attracted them. *MSF* opened an office in Malta just to handle *MOAS*."

As the 2015 season got fully underway, *MOAS* would find the need to collaborate in other ways, as they worked alongside navies from many countries, private vessels, and others to save as many lives as possible.

FROM TRAGIC SITUATION
TO UNMITIGATED CRISIS

"This weekend MOAS was involved in the rescue of more than 2,000 people from five separate migrant boats with the assistance of navy vessels from Italy, Germany, and Ireland."

With the closure of *Mare Nostrum* at the end of 2014 and the increasing misery in North Africa and Syria, everyone was braced for the spring of 2015, when migrants would once again begin fleeing their hopeless lives. It was feared the numbers willing to risk the journey might soar threefold.

In April, as the *MOAS* crew waited for their rescue mission to begin on May 1, Christopher described his feelings in a blog: *Spring has come to the Mediterranean. The days are sunny, the wind has died down, and the seas are calm. And people are dying.*

By April 20th, more than 13,500 migrants made their escape successfully, but at least five migrant boats sank in the Mediterranean killing 1200 individuals. The glaring loss of the *Mare Nostrum* project was obvious to all, and the warm season had just begun.

Malta's Prime Minister, Joseph Muscat, lashed out. "What is happening now is of epic proportions. If Europe, if the global community continues to turn a blind eye… we will all be judged in the same way that history has judged Europe when it turned a blind eye to the genocide of this century and last century."

For Christopher and the *MOAS* team, May 1st could not arrive soon enough. In their first three weeks out, in six separate rescues they rescued over 1500 individuals, among them pregnant women, young children traveling alone, babies, and young men.

Then came June, and the most intense series of rescues imaginable. The *MOAS* crew encountered an overcrowded vessel, but soon discovered another, and another, and another, with no additional rescue ships in the area. Their press release described the scene:

> *This weekend MOAS was involved in the rescue of more than 2,000 people from five separate migrant boats with the assistance of navy vessels from Italy, Germany, and Ireland. After spending several hours providing immediate assistance as the only boat on site and then more hours coordinating the rescue efforts with others, the M.Y. Phoenix is currently on its way to Sicily to disembark some 372 people including 184 men, 126 women and 62 minors, mostly from Eritrea.*

Clearly, it was a harrowing experience, but one that saved the lives of 2000 souls. It was also complex. Marco Cauchi, the captain they met on the yacht who heads the Search and Rescue efforts, told the press:

"We had to bring all our assets to bear and work diligently for many hours. I have been conducting SAR [search and rescue] in the central Mediterranean for many years, and I can say this has been one of the most intense operations because of the sheer number of people and boats in distress."

The rescue season continue unabated. By December of 2015, *MOAS* had saved 11,685 lives in two seasons of operation, for a total of just eight months.

FUNDRAISING

"Bill Gates probably wouldn't touch this with a ten–foot pole, because it has a political side to it as far as the refugees go. It could be a risk to his other global projects."

When Christopher and Regina Catrambone decided to donate $8 million to buy and retrofit the *Phoenix*, they felt confident they could raise the money to fund the operation. They didn't have a backup reserve of cash.

"That was nearly all of our savings. We aren't sitting around with $100 million."

That left them on the hook for a huge monthly cost for salaries, fuel, and a long list of other expenses. The real kicker, though, are the drones, at a cost of $300,000 a month. Yet it's the drones that make them effective, that make the work possible.

Even the life-saving, one million dollar infusion from Doctors without Borders didn't cover the high payment for the drones. Christopher had to get creative, and take further financial risk than he already had.

"The way I set up *MOAS* is that one of my companies administrates the non-profit. I didn't have that money to get the drones, which cost us $300,000 a month to operate. Doctors Without Borders gave us $1 million to operate the *Phoenix* for six months. I own the *Phoenix*, so I didn't have payments. I said, 'Let's take half that million and pay for two months of drones while we try to raise money for the rest of the operation.'

"So, I am leveraging money, and NGO's don't normally leverage. We are extremely transparent about how we operate. But we want to win out there on the water. We want to do everything possible to save lives. There is no stopping us. Of course, I am freaking out my financial guys here. They are screaming about it. 'We have to cover that cost!' But I am saying, 'Guys, we need to save lives. And it's my company, and my decision.' Tangiers is a decent size company and I don't usually micromanage. These guys are professional, and highly technical. But here I just had to say, 'We will raise more money to find a way to operate, but we are going to use these drones and kick this off with the right stuff.' It's their job to grumble at me so that's fine. I just tell them, 'If we go out without drones we won't be nearly as effective, so what's the point?'"

The fundraising was more difficult than they may have thought at the out-set. "I have learned that donors don't like to fund action-related projects. There is the liability of their own reputation. Bill Gates wouldn't touch this with a ten–foot pole, because it has a political side to it as far as the refugees go. It could be a risk to his other global projects.

"The Catrambone family is the founder of *MOAS*. We are not the end all. We don't want people to think of *MOAS* as our family. We kick started this, planning for society to take over. It should be in public hands. We funded it ourselves the first year, and used all our money. We don't have more money to spend. We can barely maintain the boat. So this will only continue if society wants it to continue. We can't force anyone to continue it. But we have proven that it can be done, that one family can change the course of history and make a huge impact."

THE WORLD FINALLY WAKES UP

"The haunting image of Aylan's body face down on the Turkish beach was powerful, and humanized the crisis for the first time for millions of people."

On September 22, 2015, the horrific image of a three-year old Syrian boy lying dead at the beach's edge shook the world. The boy, named Aylan, his older brother, Galip, their mother, and nine others drowned when the 15-foot boat they were fleeing in capsized. Their father had paid smugglers $4,500 to get his family to safety, but when the seas became rough, the Turkish smugglers abandoned the 15-foot boat, and within an hour it capsized. Their father tried to keep each of his family members adrift for hours, but slowly, as he moved from one to the other to hold them up, each eventually drowned. Devastated by grief, he would spend three more hours of agony in the water before finally being picked up by the Greek coast guard.

At once, the world came to care about the refugee crisis. The haunting image of Aylan's body face down on the Turkish beach was powerful, and humanized the crisis for the first time for millions of people. Donations suddenly flooded in, as the humanity of the crisis hit home. Within a couple of months *MOAS* announced an expansion of its operations. In addition to patrolling the Mediterranean Sea, they began operations in the Aegean Sea where two new rescue boats have begun operations to rescue the rising number of immigrants.

The names of those rescue boats? Aylan and Galip, in honor of the two young boys whose lives and deaths woke up the world.

In addition, the *Phoenix* was deployed to South East Asia for the winter, where it was put into operation to save lives in the Andaman Sea where another migrant crisis is stealing thousands of lives. Not only did the *Phoenix* rescue migrants there, *MOAS* also began to shed light on another unfolding human crisis.

NEXT STEPS

"There are other locations where the problem exists, too, like the horn of Africa, and in Yemen. The big monster is Australia, with migrants from Papua New Guinea crossing over the waters to get there, and then being put into camps when they arrive."

It's clear to everyone involved that the current rescue situation is merely a Band-aid, and that a real and lasting solution to the migrant crisis is required. The best and most permanent course is the most difficult—changing the conditions in Africa and the Middle East that drive migration, especially ending the war in Syria and across the Middle East. Supporting stable governments and building healthy economic situations is a solution the outside world could help bring about. Simply opening trade between North Africa and Europe would be a boon to African economies. However, real change in governments, policy, and politics will likely take a generation or more.

In the meantime, Christopher remains focused on saving as many lives as possible.

"I will tell you that my goal is to get more and more ships. The more ships we have, the more lives we can save. And you know what, I know in my heart I could solve this whole problem with enough ships. So, if they don't put me in jail or something", he says, jesting, "I will continue to get more ships. We have a concept that's proven. The more people we can get involved with us, the more ships we'll get out, and the more lives we'll save.

"The situation in the Mediterranean is one of the worst right now, but there are other locations where the problem exists, too, like the horn of Africa, and in Yemen. The big monster is Australia, with migrants from Papua New Guinea crossing over the waters to get there, and then being put into camps when they arrive. Then you have similar situations in the Caribbean, such as Haiti, and the Dominican Republic; and you have Cuba."

THE LONG VIEW

"When we encounter them on the sea, it is the first time in their ordeal they have been welcomed and greeted by people who wanted to be there to help them."

Despite his intensive, hands-on approach, Christopher occasionally steps back and takes in the bigger picture.

"I am a very long-term-view kind of person. *MOAS* is a very deep concept that goes beyond the physical rescues. It is meant to humanize people at sea who are dying. People need to understand what it means to drown."

Which leads to the last clue of why this work is so compelling to Christopher.

"When I was about 12 years old, I was swimming in the Comal River in New Braunfels, Texas when a current took me under. I knew I was going to die—I knew this was it. All of a sudden, like an act of God, a hand came down in the water and grabbed me and pulled me up. I was choking and coughing up water. When I calmed down, I saw it was a kid my own age who had saved me. I just hugged him, as if to say, 'Thank God you were there!' I just remember how grateful I felt."

Christopher never really connected the dots before…nearly drowning as a child, then losing his home in New Orleans and feeling like a refugee who couldn't return.

"It is very subconscious. This is not something I planned that much, and I guess I am lucky that I don't have to explain myself to too many people! I didn't plan it or think about it in that way. I know I am a doer. I just see things that need doing and I do them. I don't think about why I do it.

"I know I care about people. The difference between what we do, as a private organization, and what government rescues have done, is that we treat so-called 'migrants' like human beings. When we encounter them on the sea, it is the first time in their ordeal they have been welcomed and greeted by people who wanted to be there to help them. Last year we brought in a woman who sits on our board. She is a Harvard PhD, and she taught the crew how to be extremely sensitive with certain populations. We cannot deny them any rights. By the time they leave our boat, anywhere from 6 hours to 3 days later, every person is smiling.

"The governments can take all the time they want discussing the 'migrant problem'. In the meantime, we'll be telling the world about this, and we'll see who gets the job done. We aren't going to allow citizens to die at sea because of immigration policies. So if they can get the job done, fine, but we are going to continue striving along. We are going to be out there raising as much awareness as we can, getting more ships, and saving many, many more lives."

Afterword

The moving accounts you have just read are symbolic of a sea change, perhaps of evolutionary proportions. Whether that's reflective of how vast our current problems are, or more optimistically, a sign that we are finally taking the reigns from institutions and systems that are failing to do what's best for society, the fact is that there are more small groups forming to change the status quo than at any time in history. The sheer number of individuals setting out to resolve major and minor issues alike is unprecedented. Society is making a shift from passive acceptance to active resistance. Movement has shifted from saying, "That's just the way it is," to "That's not the way it should be and I'm going to help change it."

This is good news. We just need more of it—seven billion times more. Yet, even if 1% of the world's population began taking decisive steps to make this world better, the ripple effect would yield significant results. That's still 70 million of us, and we aren't there yet.

Reading the stories of individuals who have significantly changed the world can be both inspiring and intimidating— most of us want the world to change—but few of us see ourselves as the ones to initiate or sustain that change.

Where do you start? One place to begin is by letting the tiniest bit of awareness sneak past the powerful gatekeepers of your heart, mind, and soul. That moment we cease to ignore the cries from around the planet, from other humans, from the animals, from the oceans, the rainforests, and the air; that moment when we decide we will no longer close our eyes, turn our heads, or pass the buck is the moment we come alive; it's the moment we can no longer not act.

That act can be the slightest effort. It may mean holding the door for a person you might normally fear or dismiss. A smile can change the world.

That act may seem miniscule. It's not. It's an opening.

What is amazing to discover is that once we take the smallest action, we begin to think of ourselves as a person who works for change—as a person who is part of the solution. When we take a step to change or impact just one thing about the world around us, we begin to relax. We join the effort. We are no longer separate from it, nor separate from the world. We release the pain of blocking it all out. Once the pressure of resistance is released ever so slightly, we can think more rationally, act more decisively. Until that moment, the pressure to blot out every negative thing in the world is building in each of us whether we recognize it or not.

By intentionally helping one tiny piece of this universe, you help yourself. When you rescue one insect, recycle one bottle, smile at one stranger, you feel it. You are recognizing that you are indeed part of the whole. That simple realization begins to chip away at the protective shield that surrounds each of us and that small choice of acceptance changes everything.

LEARN MORE ABOUT THESE CHANGE MAKERS

Not everybody is meant to drop everything and go out and start a non-profit or a movement. The change makers in this book did the things that made sense to them given their interests, talents, time, age, health, and life situations.

Everyone has a role to play. Your job is to find your role. It may be volunteering an hour a week or a month for a cause you care about. It may mean financially supporting those able to do the work. It may be sharing information with others. Every effort matters, no matter how big or how small it may seem to you. The important thing is to start. Today. Read more about one of the topics presented in this book, or follow your own interests.

If you would like to volunteer, donate, or in some other way help the efforts of the organizations in this book, start by visiting their websites, listed below.

Websites for One Person Acted Change Makers

KATIE MEYLER-MORE THAN ME FOUNDATION
Getting Girls Off the Street and into School in Liberia, West Africa
www.morethanme.org

SCOTLUND HAISLEY—ANIMAL RESCUE CORPS
Ending animal suffering through direct and compassionate action
www.animalrescuecorps.org

PAUL POLAK—WINDHORSE INTERNATIONAL AND IDE
Revolutionizing design to serve the world's poorest people
www.paulpolak.com
www.ideorg.org

LOUIE PSIHOYOS—OCEANIC PRESERVATION SOCIETY
Exposing complex environmental issues and promoting advocacy
www.opsociety.org

SHARON CONTENT—CHILDREN OF PROMISE
Empowering children of incarcerated parents to break the cycle
www.cpnyc.org

NATHAN RUNKLE—MERCY FOR ANIMALS
Ending cruelty to farmed animals
www.mercyforanimals.org

RAED MUALEM—NAZARETH ACADEMIC INSTITUTE
A bridge to peace: securing higher education for arabs in israel
www.raedmualem.org

BERNARD AMADEI—ENGINEERS WITHOUT BORDERS USA
Engineering for change
www.ewb-usa.org

RABINDRA MISHRA—HELP NEPAL
Restoring the soul of nepal
www.helpnepal.net

CHRISTOPHER CATRAMBONE—MIGRANT OFFSHORE AID STATION
Saving lives at sea: the world's most dangerous border crossing
www.moas.eu

Thank you for joining me on this journey. I hope you will continue to follow my work and share your experiences with me.

WEBSITE
www.onepersonacted.com

FACEBOOK
www.facebook.com/onepersonacted

EMAIL
deborah@onepersonacted.com

ACKNOWLEDGEMENTS

My sincerest thanks go first and foremost to those individuals I interviewed for this book, including many whose stories do not appear on these pages due to practical limits. Your stories are equally inspiring and will all be shared in some form. I thank each of you for your commitment to living for something bigger than yourself. I thank you for taking a stand, for giving your all, for showing the way, for being the change.

My heartfelt thanks and deepest gratitude go to my co-author, Ricky Schlueter. Your excellent writing skills, powerful insight, inspirational company, and relentless dedication to the book's message are the reason it reached publication. You kept me focused and on track. Your powerful influence on this book shows up in every word, as well as in how you live your life every day. I thank you with a full and grateful heart.

Many, many thanks to Jack Canfield for writing the foreword to this book, and for teaching me all I needed to know about living my purpose fully.

Incalculable thanks to my daughter, Jessica Schlueter, for connecting me with many of the world changers in this book. Without your fervent interest and continual support for this project, it simply would not have materialized. Thanks, also, for noticing the coffee stain on the airplane tray, and gifting me the solution.

Diane (Morris) Southard devoted endless hours to transcribing interviews, building a website, and supporting the ideas and motivation behind this book and its related work. Thank you for your collaboration, dedication, and friendship.

Sincere thanks to my former student, Birendra Dhakal, for calling my attention to the situation in Nepal and connecting me to Rabindra Mishra.

Compared to the joy of interviewing and writing, the laborious task of editing is my least favorite part of book writing. Thanks here go to many, but the lion's share must be showered on Rick Schlueter. Your eagle eye for grammar, spelling, and punctuation is a godsend, as were the many hours you spent reviewing every word, space and comma. I appreciate you and your help in editing.

Muffy Albada provided valuable last-minute story advice that resulted in small but important material changes. Thank you for being diligent. Sharon Campbell, you also gave excellent editing advice, and as always were generous with your time and caring spirit. Thanks also to Diane Larson for your daily support for the book, and for your lifetime of friendship.

Thanks to Chris Hoar for your vote of confidence early on, and for taking the photographs that appear on the back cover. I deeply appreciate your support.

Perhaps the greatest help anyone can give a writer is moral support. For this I am blessed to have many helpers, especially my siblings, Laurie Staples, Robert Rohan, Kathy Hague, and Muffy Albada, who together prove family is our bedrock and our shield. I especially thank our late brother, Mike Rohan, who always helped make dreams come true. This book is among those dreams.

I want to thank my friends who have always believed in me and supported my efforts no matter what direction they take. At the risk of leaving someone out I won't mention all your names, but you know who you are and I thank you with all my heart. You make this ride fun.

Finally, thanks to my dearest friend, poet Tom McCoy. You left this world too early, but your writing counsel still finds its way onto my page every day.

ABOUT THE AUTHOR

The author of several published articles and two books, Deborah Rohan is also a professional speaker, trainer, and coach. She is the founder of One Person Acted, which guides individuals and organizations to consider their impact on the world, encouraging them to become conscious, committed world changers as they fully live out their own life purpose.

Deborah's message is enriched by 25 years experience bringing diverse cultures together, first as conflict mediator and diversity trainer, and later working to improve relationships between the West and the Middle East through leading dialogue and shared experiences. She served as Executive Director of two non-profits, including a Middle East center at a major university, and a non-profit she co-founded dedicated to building peace between East and West.

Deborah is a certified trainer of *The Success Principles*™, having been personally taught by Jack Canfield, one of the world's top transformational leaders and author of *The Success Principles*™. As part of this elite group of trainers, she collaborates with fellow certified trainers to present workshops locally, nationally, and globally.

She is a trained facilitator for *Awakening the Dreamer Symposium*, created by the Pachamama Alliance, a global community working together to usher in a more sustainable and socially just world for all.

For more information about One Person Acted's training and coaching, or to inquire about hiring Deborah as a speaker, contact her office at:

One Person Acted

1031 3 3rd Street, Denver, Colorado, USA 80205
Email: info@onepersonacted.com
Website: www.onepersonacted.com
Phone: 970-205-9120
Facebook: facebook.com/OnePersonActed/